Abul Asar Hafeez Jalandhari

A REVOLUTIONARY AND REVERED POET LAUREATE'S TIMELESS LEGACY

Abul Asar Hafeez Jalandhari

A REVOLUTIONARY AND REVERED POET LAUREATE'S TIMELESS LEGACY

Naveen Khan

ISBN 978-1-0688348-2-0 - *Digital*
ISBN 978-1-0688348-1-3 - *Paperback*
ISBN 978-1-0688348-0-6 - *Hardcover*

Book Design by Marko Markovic, 5mediadesign

Contents

Prologue

Abul Asar Hafeez Jalandhari, renowned for his literary prowess, was honored with the titles "Khan" and "Khan Bahadur" by the British Indian government for his invaluable service during the Second World War. However, guided by the vision of the nation's founder, Mohammad Ali Jinnah, he willingly surrendered these titles.

Abhi To Main Jawan Hun
(I Am Still Young)

The air is delightful, the flowers are in bloom,
There's a melody in the air, Spring is in full swing.
Where has the cupbearer gone? Come back, come back this way.
Look, who is watching? The dawn is breaking slowly.
Rise, rise, O cupbearer! Fill the cup, fill it and bring it here,
Turn your gaze towards the garden, look at the ambiance, be aware.
Look at those dark clouds, they have gathered on the horizon.

It's a gathering of wine drinkers, the wine house is in full swing.
What arrogance is this, so disdainful? Understand me, O ignorant one.
The idea of asceticism, where is it now? I am still young.
The mention of worship is there, concern for salvation too,
Passion has its rewards; the thought is a torment.

This wandering, searching, this exploration of heights,
The chirping of nightingales, the laughter of the flower-faced ones.
If there is a connection with someone, worries and thoughts are lost,
Sometimes when destiny sleeps, the one who laughs starts crying.

Hafeez Jalandhari

Hafeez Jalandhari was conferred with the prestigious "Pride of Performance" award and the esteemed "Hilal-e-Imtiaz" for his unparalleled literary contributions by the government of Pakistan.

Foreword

Tribute to Grandfather

By Naveen Khan (Granddaughter)

Intricately woven into the fabric of destiny, the mantle of preserving my grandfather's legacy fell upon my shoulders—a task unbeknownst to me until the wheels of fate set it in motion. Little did I anticipate the profound journey that awaited, a journey that would be unveiled through the lens of his captivating work.

The catalysts of this endeavor were not mere artifacts; they were precious fragments of a rich narrative handed down to me. My mother entrusted me with a trove of his cherished photographs, urging me to immortalize them within the pages of an album. Alongside this, my aunts Zia and Shameem contributed an invaluable assortment of materials—audio tapes and transcripts meticulously curated.

As I embarked on a new chapter in North America, a letter surfaced, a poignant reminder of the responsibility that now rested upon me. It lay dormant, patiently awaiting its turn to influence the narrative.

It was not until the turbulent waves of a global pandemic forced me into solitude, that I sought solace in these relics. The materials, once scattered, gradually came to form a cohesive tapestry, weaving the threads of my grandfather's life into a compelling biography.

This two-year odyssey, a labor of love and dedication, reached its crescendo as I stumbled upon a letter from him (below) —a fitting finale to the culmination of his extraordinary tale.

My grandfather, Hafeez Jalandhari, had taken me under his wing from birth. It was said that I was a mere newborn when I first arrived to share a home with him and my grandmother, providing assistance to my young parents within an extended family tradition.

A Grandfather's Wish Honoured

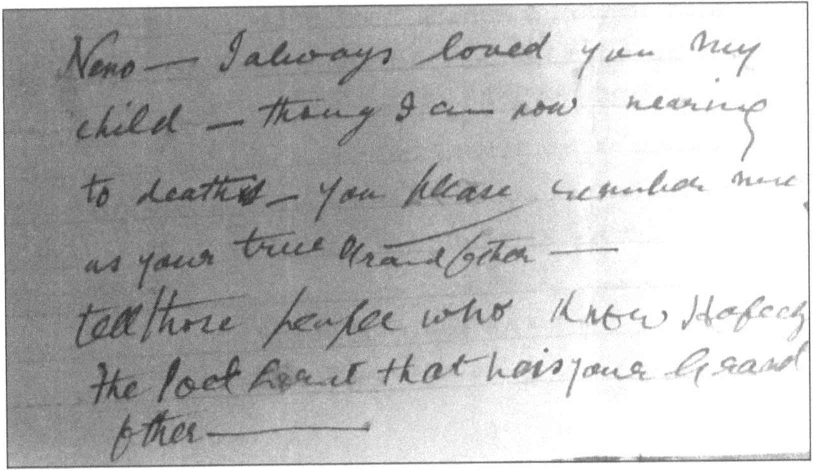

Neno- I always loved you my child- though I am now nearing to death- you please remember me as your true Grandfather-Tell those people who know Hafeez the Poet Laureate that he is your Grandfather.

I fondly remember the mornings spent in his writing room, enveloped by the comforting scent of well-worn books mingling with the aromatic swirls of his hookah. His bed had papers strewn all across it, a testament to his penchant for sitting amidst written chaos, penning his thoughts.

This creative journey was intricately intertwined with the crucial influence of my grandparents. Long after my grandfather's passing, his work, words, and wisdom continued to reverberate in my soul, becoming a lifeline that kept me alive. In the changing tides of the world and the global pandemic crisis, the sense of belonging fostered by his legacy provided an anchor.

His teachings have transcended time, offering solace and guidance in a tumultuous world. The creative flame he ignited within me became a resilient beacon, guiding me through the darkest hours and echoing in the verses of my music.

In the tapestry of his influence, I found not only the inspiration for my art but a profound connection that has withstood the tests of time and adversity.

Naveen Khan
Grand daughter of Hafeez Jalandhari
Teacher, Musician, Songwriter and Recording artist.

Preface

Unveiling Hafeez Jalandhari's Legacy

Hafeez Jalandhari's biography is a compelling testament to his remarkable life journey, capturing the essence of a poet, a patriot, and a visionary. As the chapters unfold, it is abundantly clear that his legacy is not confined to the pages of this book; it resonates deeply with readers and admirers alike, making his life story both outstanding and relatable.

The chapters weave together the threads of Hafeez Jalandhari's life, his cultural and literary contributions, and his impact on the world stage. It leaves one with a profound understanding that his life was not just a personal journey, but a universal odyssey, reflecting the shared human experience of unwavering dedication to art and the pursuit of excellence. It can be seen as an invitation, to inspire and uplift the world through one's own unique passions and talents.

The placement of his biography within the broader context of his contributions to literature, culture, and his homeland Pakistan elevates the biography to another level. It serves as a bridge connecting readers to the rich tapestry of history, culture, and patriotism. This resonance transforms Hafeez Jalandhari from a distant figure in history to a relatable icon, someone whose dreams, struggles, and triumphs can inspire anyone to strive for greatness.

The conclusion underscores the enduring relevance of his work and his profound impact on Pakistan's identity. Hafeez Jalandhari's legacy isn't confined by borders; it extends a warm invitation to everyone to embrace the shared human experience. It highlights the universal themes in his poetry, which continue to inspire, uplift, and resonate with readers worldwide. His legacy endures as a beacon of hope, a symbol of unity, and a treasure of the literary world, demonstrating the boundless potential of the written word to transcend boundaries and unite humanity.

In a world divided by boundaries, Hafeez Jalandhari's biography is a reminder that great men like him, through their work and their words, can inspire and connect people across the globe. He is a testament to the timeless power of literature and the indomitable spirit of humanity, inviting all to find a unique voice and leave a legacy that transcends time and place.

Ultimately, Hafeez Jalandhari's biography serves as a rallying call to all readers, urging them to embrace their unique journeys, to be inspired by the universal truths from his life story, and to believe that their own stories can become a source of inspiration and unity for generations to come.

A Poet and Humanitarian

I

Ancestry, City of Jalandhar, India

1

Tracing Roots
in Time's Tapestry

In the vibrant world of poetry, Hafeez Jalandhari emerges as a figure whose words possess the enchanting power to transcend temporal and spatial confines, weaving a tapestry that resonates with the echoes of history. A luminary among literary constellations, he beckons us into a realm where verses embody, not only passion and wisdom, but also an intricate connection to a bygone era of grandeur and conquest. Delving into the roots of the poet's lineage and setting forth on a journey to the ancient city of Jalandhar, the footprints of Alexander the Great can still be traced upon the historical canvas.

The ancient city of Jalandhar, dating back to 100 A.D., stands as a silent witness to the ebb and flow of empires, notably marked by the conquest of Alexander in 326 BC. The battlegrounds in this region, where the clash of mighty forces unfolded, echo with the resonance of an era that shaped the course of history.

Centuries unfurl, revealing the ascendancy and decline of ruling powers. The Mughals, in 1188, established a Muslim dynasty, and the governance of twelve villages surrounding Jalandhar fell under the sway of Pathan chiefs, warriors known for their prowess and dignified demeanor. However, their internal strife weakened the Muslim rule, and wove more conflict into the city's narrative.

The 19th century ushered in a new chapter as Maharaja Ranjit Singh assumed dominion over Punjab, heralding the rise of the Sikh Empire. Under his rule, the influence of the twelve chiefs waned, and Jalandhar's industries thrived, notably in wood carving and lock-manufacturing—endeavors monopolized by Ud Muslims and Hindus, respectively.

Against this historical backdrop, near an ancient graveyard, resided a family with a fascinating lineage. Originally Hindu Rajputs, they had embraced Islam, and the family's patriarch undertook a pilgrimage to Mecca. His final resting place there marked the genesis of a legacy, leaving behind three sons, including Mehr-ud-Din. Mehr-ud-Din and his brothers embarked on a prosperous business supplying firearms, uniforms, and provisions to the troops. However, the political turbulence in Punjab during that era presented challenges, with local intrigues and the loss of patronage impacting their prosperity. Yet, the family resiliently preserved its belongings and heritage.

The turning point in Jalandhar's history materialized in 1844, following Maharaja Ranjit Singh's demise. The collapse of the Sikh kingdom paved the way for the British conquest, and amidst the shadows of cantonments, Mehr-ud-Din discerned an opportunity to rebuild his life. Thriving in trade with British troops and police, he secured a license to sell sulfur and salt-peter. While not amassing opulence, Mehr-ud-Din and his kin lived as esteemed citizens, contributing a chapter to the city's evolving tale.

Legacy of Resilience - The Ancestry and Ascent of Poet Hafeez Jalandhari

The family lineage of the poet Hafeez Jalandhari can be traced back to his grandfather, Mehr-ud-Din, who had two sons, Shams-ud-Din and Shahab-ud-Din. While Shams-ud-Din was involved in business and had his own family, Shahab-ud-Din was known for his intellect and mastery of Persian, Arabic, and Urdu. Tragically, Shahab-ud-Din's life took a turn for the worse when he passed away, leaving behind his wife, Batul, and their two sons and infant daughter.

Despite their Muslim faith, the family adhered to Hindu Rajput customs and traditions. Concerned about Batul remarrying and potentially losing her dowry, they made an unconventional decision—Batul would be married to Shams-ud-Din as his second wife, a practice allowed by the Quran but with conditions. Initially hesitant, Batul was convinced to accept this arrangement for the security it provided to her and her children.

Unfortunately, this decision led to further troubles. Shams-ud-Din's first wife and her children treated Batul and her children from her first marriage with cruelty and resentment. Despite enduring these hardships with patience, Batul and her children faced further conflicts when Mehr-ud-Din arranged marriages between two of Batul's sons and two daughters from the first marriage, worsening tensions within the family.

Amidst these hardships, Batul maintained her gentle demeanor, despite facing hostility and jealousy from others. As she endured their wrath, she discovered she was expecting a child with Shams-ud-Din, which only intensified the jealousy of the first wife, compounding Batul's pain and anguish. Desperate and overwhelmed by her circumstances, Batul yearned for relief. However, fate had other plans.

Despite facing immense adversity, she gave birth to a son named Mohammed Hafeez, who would later become a prominent literary figure in the Indian subcontinent. Their lives would be further shaped by the partition of the country in 1947, leading to the creation of India and Pakistan. Hafeez carried forward a legacy of resilience, empathy, and artistic brilliance. His mother's struggles only fueled his determination to give voice to the oppressed and advocate for justice through his poetry.

Hafeez's journey from a turbulent beginning to becoming one of the most celebrated literary figures in pre-partition India, now Pakistan, serves as a testament to the enduring spirit of human perseverance and creativity.

Young Hafeez reciting at Jubilee Brigadier Gulzar Ahmed present 1950, Pakistan.

II

Early Life

2

The Birth of an Iconic Poet Laureate

On a fateful day, January 14th, in the year 1900, the world witnessed the arrival of a special soul, Mohammed Hafeez, with an aura of destiny surrounding him. At his birth, two exceptional women, moved by a profound sense of moral duty, stood by his mother's side. One was the wife of Karam Bakhsh, a cousin of the child's grandfather, and the other, Hasna, his brother's widow. Given the nature of the family's complexities, they offered unwavering support, recognizing the need to heal old wounds. These two remarkable women, wealthy but without children of their own, were destined for a higher purpose.

While the birth announcement brought forth familial tensions, the compassion and wisdom displayed by Hasna, her brother, and sister-in-law were extraordinary. They chose to embrace the child as their own, seeing an opportunity to mend the broken bonds of the family. With an open heart, Hasna approached the child's father, proposing to adopt the new-born. Her genuine plea was met with warmth and acceptance, sealing the fate of the young poet in the most unexpected but loving hands.

Under the care of Hasna and her kin, the child was immersed in love and devotion from the start. The first call to prayer echoed in his ears, reminding him of the divine presence in his life. Overflowing with pride and joy, Hasna summoned religious men and Mullahs to recite the holy Quran in celebration of the child's arrival. The courtyard brimmed with happiness as relatives and friends joined in heartfelt congratulations. In this atmosphere of unbridled joy, the child flourished, his heart forever touched by the love and care surrounding him.

As he grew into a poet, those cherished memories remained etched in his soul. The contented voices of women, the tender embraces, and the feeling of belonging to a larger family all shaped his artistic spirit. Amid the bustling days, Hafeez's adop-tive father, Karam Bakhsh, reveled in his role as a parent. Together, they frequented his rug shop, where the child's innocent babbling brought smiles to all who heard. The shop became a haven of shared happiness, where dreams and imag-ination thrived.

In moments of reflection, the poet revisited the past, remem-bering his mother's hardships and how, in his innocent way, he tried to console her. Filled with love, he resolved to fulfill all her unmet wishes when he grew up.

Young Hafeez reciting at Jubilee
1950, Pakistan.

III

Formative Years

3

Education and Influences

Hafeez embarked on his educational journey at the tender age of four years and four months. He was ceremoniously introduced to his first Quranic lesson, dressed in resplendent silks and satins. A round cap, intricately embroidered in gold, graced his head, and his eyes appeared conspicuously large, accentuated with surma, a traditional eyeliner. This momentous occasion was graced by his father and other relatives as they guided him to the nearest mosque, a sacred place endowed by his forefathers.

In those times, it was customary for Muslim children to commence their Quranic education at the age of four. These mosques, besides being centers of prayer, also functioned as schools, harkening back to a time when the mosque was the cradle of Islamic knowledge.

Upon entering the mosque's hall, Hafeez was greeted with a sight that etched itself into his memory forever. Two trays of sweet spherical laddoos, a traditional sweet, adorned the scene, and a gathering of boys sat on mats with legs crossed. Each child had a wooden stand before them, known as a Rihl, upon which they fervently recited the Quran, swaying their bodies in rhythm. Facing this youthful assembly was the Mulla, mirroring the posture of the children, clutching a cane in his lap.

As Hafeez entered, the Mulla rose to extend his warm welcome, causing the other children to converge around the new pupil, their faces lit with anticipation of sweets and a day off from studies. After the initial hubbub, the Mulla calmed the excited crowd and proceeded to invoke prayers over the laddoos, creating a sacred hush over the gathering. With arms raised in reverence, the children stood, their souls absorbed in the sacred mystique of the moment. For Hafeez, this experience was overwhelming, a vision he had never before witnessed, and one that would leave an indelible mark on his heart.

After beseeching blessings upon the traditional sweet, the Mulla selected one, took a bite, and then graciously handed the remainder to Hafeez. The rest of the laddoos were subsequently shared among the children, some finding their way into Hafeez's handkerchief, while the rest were distributed among his family members.

Following this initiation ceremony, Hafeez received his first Quranic lesson, though the children were more enamored with the announcement that followed which meant a holiday for the students. An older boy was assigned the responsibility of escorting Hafeez to and from school, and the rest of the boys were granted a holiday.

Hafeez quickly settled into his new routine. Alongside his classmates, he undertook the task of maintaining the mosque's cleanliness, a duty assigned to the students. The townsfolk rallied together to support the destitute who resided within the mosque's confines. Hafeez, along with several other boys, diligently collected food and alms, which they presented to the Mulla for equitable distribution among the less fortunate. This charitable act became a daily ritual.

Yet, like all children, Hafeez occasionally exhibited disobedience, for which he faced reprimand. The form of punishment was, at times, lightheartedly amusing. The disobedient child would be instructed to stand with his head wedged between his knees, clutching his ears from behind his legs. This predicament proved too tempting for his mischievous peers, who, when the Mulla's watchful eye wavered, would subtly push him, temporarily liberating him from his plight. Such actions often resulted in a growing group of boys standing in identical positions. They patiently awaited the intervention of outsiders, who would peer in and request the Mulla to release them, a request they undoubtedly welcomed.

Punishments and lessons were not the sole components of their school experience. During the winter months, the boys found joy in the simple pleasures, such as roasting corn. Taking their corn to a local shop for roasting, they generously shared a portion with the shopkeeper before placing the corn into a sizable roasting pan filled with hot sand, nestled within a fire pit dug into the ground. They would then tuck the corn into their shirt laps and invite the Mulla to partake in this corn feast. The Mulla, never one to decline such invitations, would bless the corn, and together, they would savor a modest banquet.

Women in those days very often used to hold, female-only, religious meetings in different houses in the city as that was the only occasion when they could meet each other socially. Such meetings dealt with different topics, the main being religious. Some women were selected at each meeting to recite parts of the Koran, as well as poems in praise of the Prophet Mohammed.

Hafeez loved attending these meetings and took a childish delight in reciting when he got up on the platform to sing and recite from the Holy Koran. The small attractive boy enchanted the audience: he endeared himself to all with his sincerity and earnestness. He convinced the congregation that he would one day be a servant and worker of Islam.

For two years, Hafeez diligently attended lessons at the mosque, emerging as an exceptionally bright student. He learned to recite portions of the Quran from memory and read from the holy book, even though, due to his tender age, the profound meanings eluded him. He also acquired the rudiments of Arabic and Persian, and his curriculum even included the works of Saadi, the renowned Persian poet. Even in his youth, Hafeez garnered praise as an exemplary student, promising a bright future ahead.

After two years at the Mosque, the boy's adoptive parents felt that it was no longer necessary for him to continue his religious studies. He had learnt all that was needed from the religious point of view. They intended to send him to school for attainment of secular education. When the last day approached for him to take the last lesson at the mosque, everything was arranged. Sweetmeats, clothes, and a turban were offered with fifty-one rupees to the Mullah, which he placed in the courtyard of the mosque. Children and the parting pupil with his relatives gathered around and joined in prayer that was recited over these gifts.

When the Mulla finished his prayers, he put his hand on the boy's head, blessed him, and gave him guidance for his future journey in life. Young Hafeez saw tears roll down the Mulla's cheeks onto his long white sacred beard. The blessing guided the poet in all he undertook to do; the gentle words spoken to an innocent child had a lasting effect, even if they did not at the time of hearing. Tears were noticed in the eyes of the poet when he later spoke of this.

The beauty and truth of such a lesson, no doubt, guided him throughout his life. The poet's last lesson at the mosque was over. His friends gathered around, embracing him. They shook hands and said goodbyes to a friend whose fate was to lead him on the path of fame, though also accompanied by severe hardships and hunger.

Hafeez's Scholarly Voyage and Artistic Revelation

By the age of twelve, Hafeez had attended various schools, and his parents and relatives had encountered numerous challenges with him. At each school, he found their strict rules and regulations stifling his defiant spirit, prompting him to run off from one school to another.

 ABUL ASAR HAFEEZ JALANDHARI

Hafeez and Shamim Parneel at poetic gathering, Pakistan.

Hafeez's journey into the world of poetry and destiny began at the tender age of seven, during his second-grade class. At seven years old, he penned his first poem. The subject of his poetic expression was none other than the Prophet Muhammad, an unexpected inspiration that he could not explain even in hindsight.

This initial foray into poetry would later serve as the echo of a voice that had first emerged in the form of humble praise: "I will embark in the boat of Muhammad (Peace be upon him). Then my boat will reach the shore safely. Mohammed Hafeez has composed a poem; God's grace is now upon him."

In the dim light of a dark room, with a wooden pen and a board as his companions, the seven-year-old Hafeez poured his thoughts into a hundred verses. He wrote without realizing that he was crafting poetry; his words flowed with a song in his heart, filling him with a joyous elation. Although his vocabulary was limited and his language a mixture of Urdu and Punjabi, the profundity of his thoughts was undeniable, especially for a child of his age.

For an entire week, Hafeez's mind was consumed by the poem he had created. He copied it onto pieces of paper, carefully gilded the edges, and shared his creation with his friends. Yet, as quickly as it had emerged, this poem faded into obscurity after just one week, a mere glimpse of the poetic destiny that lay ahead.

During his school days, Hafeez formed a deep friendship with one of his classmates. For three or four years, they were inseparable, sharing not only their joys but also their mischievous escapades and the consequences of their defiance. Hafeez was fortunate to have some pocket money provided by his parents, which proved handy during their adventures and the times they evaded school. After some time Hafeez and his friend grew apart leaving Hafeez to explore his destiny.

While it wasn't uncommon for Hafeez to wander away from home, his prolonged absences consistently stirred anxiety among his family. On one particular occasion, he had been away for a staggering four months, resulting in a reprimand upon his return, a punishment that subdued him temporarily. Despite facing consequences, Hafeez retained a defiant, untamed nature. His propensity for mischief coexisted with intellectual ambitions, demonstrating a precocious development of his imagination.

Hafeez, possessed by a deep love for literature, often found solace in books, immersing himself in intellectual pursuits. His understanding of complex concepts set him apart, making it challenging for him to engage with his peers on a casual level. His mind, a constant whirlwind of thoughts, gravitated toward profound subjects that occupied the minds of great men.

Whenever the opportunity arose, Hafeez delved into the realms of literature, finding contentment miles away from the familiar surroundings of home. In the countryside, he would sit on the grass, drawing inspiration from nature, relishing moments when he could feel his sole human existence from these pursuits. Hafeez cherished solitude, reveling in the melodies of birds, the whispers of trees, and the gentle murmurs of streams, all accompanied by the fragrance of fresh earth and blooming flowers.

If given the chance, Hafeez would have willingly secluded himself amidst the beauty and pleasures of nature, distancing himself from the hustle and bustle of the human world. The happiness he derived during his childhood stemmed from pursuits that brought him joy. This theme of doing what pleased him continued throughout his life.

While Hafeez managed to avoid serious trouble, his unruly willfulness invoked deep concern in his real mother, despite their limited interactions. Her life, already a mere existence, found further complication due to her son's unpredictable nature. Hafeez's actions, although not intentionally harmful, added to the complexities of his mother's already unhappy life.

In his thirteenth year, Hafeez made a momentous decision that
would alter the course of his life forever; he ran away from
school for good. Fueling this escape was a daring act—he took a
significant sum of money from his own home. This marked the
beginning of a tumultuous period in his life, as he embarked
on a journey that would take him to several cities, including
Delhi, Meerut, Bombay, and others.

As Hafeez ventured into the unknown, he unintentionally
began to improve his knowledge of Urdu. Roaming the bust-
ling streets of Delhi and the vibrant bazaars of Meerut, he
immersed himself in the language, absorbing not just its words
but also its proper pronunciation and the authentic spirit of
its usage. He learned by listening to the conversations of the
people who spoke Urdu as their mother tongue. These informal
language lessons were an unintended, yet invaluable, part of
his self-discovery.

Meanwhile, back at home, Hafeez's worried parents launched
inquiries about his whereabouts in neighboring districts and
police stations. Little did they know that the police station in Delhi
held crucial information about their wayward son. While on his
escapade, Hafeez had drawn the attention of the authorities. He
had been generously giving away five- and ten-rupee notes to
beggars, a gesture that raised suspicions among the local police.
Concerned about the source of his funds, they apprehended him
and escorted him to the police station for questioning.

Facing the inquiries of the police, Hafeez managed to convince
them that he was not a thief and that his actions were not

criminal in nature. Perhaps it was his innocence or his ability to articulate his situation convincingly, but he succeeded in satisfying their concerns. Following this encounter, the authorities released him from custody.

This chapter concludes with Hafeez's return home, a pivotal moment that marks the end of his unintentional adventure and the beginning of a new chapter in his life. This return signifies not only the culmination of his tumultuous escapade but also sets the stage for the exploration of the various influences that shaped Hafeez's character and contributed to his development as a poet, laying the foundation for his creative journey.

Hafeez reciting a poem Burki-
27 January 1952 Lahore, Pakistan.

IV

The Poet Emerges

4

First Poetic Endeavors

As Hafeez reached the age of sixteen, his mother, noting his carefree nature, felt it was time for him to gain a deeper understanding of life and his role in the world. She considered marriage as a solution to instill a sense of responsibility in him, arranging for his union with a distant relative, a tradition already set since infancy.

Interestingly, the bride-to-be, initially unknown to Hafeez, would play a significant role in his transformative journey. His entry into marital life became a journey of self-discovery, where he grappled with life's demands and responsibilities. Within just three days of marriage, Hafeez faced opposition from his stepbrother, who resented the extended family. This resistance fueled Hafeez's determination to shield his family from insults and suffering.

Despite his unwavering resolve, Hafeez found himself without a means of earning a living and empty pockets. Undeterred, his primary focus became finding employment. However, the quest revealed the scarcity of opportunities for inexperienced individuals. Faced with disappointments, dejection, and despair, Hafeez, driven by the headstrong nature cultivated in his childhood, persevered in his pursuit of employment to support his family.

The Poet's Resilience: Navigating Loss and Discovering Hope through Verse

By the time Hafeez reached his sixteenth year, his family had weathered significant losses, casting a long shadow over their lives. Several family members, including his brothers and the woman who had lovingly raised him, Hasna, had passed away. These losses left widows and orphans, placing a substantial burden on the shoulders of Hafeez's father, Shams-ud-Din. The hallmark of this family was a profound sense of duty and unwavering dignity.

Shams-ud-Din dedicated himself to supporting these widows and orphans, irrespective of their lack of blood ties. To him, they constituted an integral part of the family, and he felt an unwavering duty to provide for them. This commitment took a toll on his nerves and overall health, leaving him easily agitated and irritable.

Meanwhile, Shams-ud-Din's first wife mourned the loss of her two sons and grew bitter. While these circumstances could have brought the two women together through shared sorrow, fate played cruel tricks on their destinies. One woman was destined to a life of perpetual sorrow, while the other's existence was tainted by bitterness. Financially, the family found itself in dire straits, descending into a pit of despair and misery.

During this tumultuous period, Hafeez began to take his poetry seriously, and the domestic turmoil indirectly influenced his creative work. He grew acutely aware of how these gloomy surroundings had left a profound mark on his psyche. His verses began to mirror the world's pervasive sorrow, unhappiness, and selfishness.

At this stage, Hafeez had no inkling that he could earn money from his writing, and, thus, he did not actively seek to publish his work. When he was sixteen, his adoptive father passed away, leaving behind three properties. Hafeez moved in with his mother, only to discover that his family harbored resentment and even hatred toward him.

They constantly reminded him of his spendthrift ways. It was true that he struggled to save money and had never fully grasped the concept of responsibility. His upbringing had left him ill-equipped for business or a career that could sustain him and his family.

Writing poetry remained his sole pursuit, one he viewed as a mere hobby. Amid the disapproval, poetry remained his solace. It was the one thing he held dear and found comfort in during these trying times. Little did he know that his passion for poetry would eventually become his path to financial stability and recognition. Yet, for the moment, his focus remained on expressing his emotions through verse, finding solace in the words that flowed from his heart and pen.

In the year 1917, against the tumultuous backdrop of the Great War, Hafeez managed to secure a job at a factory tasked with producing uniforms for the troops. His workdays were grueling, extending from six in the morning to six in the evening. In return for his toil, he received a meager salary of 25 rupees per month. Hafeez's daily routine was marked by sacrifice and endurance.

He would rise at the early hour of four in the morning, carefully wrapping his breakfast in a handkerchief before setting out on a five-mile walk to his workplace. During his journey, he would occasionally pause to enjoy a simple snack. In the evening, he would return home fatigued and weary, unable to afford the luxury of transportation. His meager earnings barely covered life's essentials, and even then, they fell short of supporting the dependents relying on him. Nevertheless, they managed as best as they could with what little they had. Hafeez found solace in knowing that he was contributing to the well-being of those who depended on him.

Unfortunately, his employment at the factory was short-lived, as his employers considered him inexperienced and terminated his contract after just three months. Although disappointed, Hafeez remained undeterred. He embarked once again on the arduous task of job hunting. After a week of searching, he secured a position with a tailor, albeit one that offered even lower wages than his previous job. Despite this setback, he chose to keep this information from his wife and mother, not wishing to burden them or reveal the difficulties he faced. Instead, he borrowed money to compensate for the diminished income and pretended that his new job represented an improvement.

However, Hafeez was not wholeheartedly committed to his work as he believed he was destined for greater things. His aspirations soared beyond the ordinary, and he yearned to achieve what seemed unattainable to others. While financial concerns weighed heavily on his mind, he felt a sense of degradation in his labor, convinced that it was not his true calling. A month later, Hafeez ventured into a new enterprise—sewing tunics—that took him far from home. He entered into a partnership with a friend, and together they managed the business for approximately 12 months.

Hafeez's Path to First Laurels

Hafeez's journey began against the morbid backdrop of the Great War, a storm raging across European countries. Amidst these uncertain times, he chanced upon a poster affixed to a wall—an invitation to all poets to participate in a mushaira, a poetic gathering where a prize awaited the poet who could craft the most profound verse on the war.

At first, Hafeez hesitated, seeing himself as a novice compared to the famous and established poets expected to participate. His self-doubt loomed large. However, a friend encouraged him to take part, planting a seed of hope in his mind. Still, he held little hope for success. Nonetheless, the idea of participating ignited a dormant spark of poetry within him. With wavering intentions, Hafeez decided to take the plunge.

As the event unfolded and he listened to the other poets, Hafeez's confidence grew. When his name was called to recite his poem, he faced not only the audience but also mockery from supposed masters of poetry—elderly poets with long beards and young but locally renowned wordsmiths. Their sly smiles and pointed fingers seemed to taunt him—a daring, audacious young poet challenging their authority; yet, Hafeez remained unfazed. As he stood up to take the stage, an unusual incident occurred. As he got ready to recite, he put on his coat, and a few coins tumbled from his pocket, scattering across the floor. The audience grew impatient, but Hafeez, undisturbed, stooped down to pick up each coin, one by one, regardless of the impatience in the room. It was as though he was unearthing his own determination.

Finally, when all his coins were safely back in his pocket, he ascended the platform to recite his poem. His verses recounted the cruelties inflicted by the Germans on Liege castle in Belgium, vividly describing the destruction and horror of a German attack. His words painted a poignant picture, and the audience was spellbound. Yet, Hafeez's poem was more than just a narrative of destruction; it was an impassioned appeal for aid to the suffering and homeless. Its originality and the forceful portrayal of his verses impressed the audience, leaving them in awe. They felt as though a new kind of poetry master had emerged, breaking free from any conventional norms.

The renowned poets who had initially mocked him now wore astonished and appreciative expressions. The judges, in agreement with the audience, unanimously chose Hafeez's poem as the winner. After eight years of writing poetry solely for his own enjoyment, he now had the joy of seeing the public appreciate his work. As a reward, Hafeez received a gold medal, a prize that left him elated. However, he pondered what to do with the medal. It was a symbol of his first laurels, a testament to his newfound recognition. Eventually, he made a decision that brought the story to a heartwarming conclusion.

Hafeez took the medal to a goldsmith, requesting that it be melted down and fashioned into a pair of earrings. His impatience and excitement were palpable as he waited at the shop. Upon returning home, he presented the medal, now transformed into earrings, intended for his wife to his mother. The story of the earrings surprised his family, as they had been unaware of his participation in the contest.

Word of Hafeez's achievement reached his father and others, who congratulated him on having such a brilliant son. However, his family, unable to appreciate the value and beauty of poetry, thought of poets as madmen. During this time in the Punjab, poetry held little appreciation, and writers derived no substantial benefit unless they were connected to the courts of native states.

Hafeez, after having seen the result of the contest, began to feel that his poetry should be the aim of his life. He decided to spend more time on it. The incident at the poetic gathering marked a turning point in his life. His journey in the world of poetry continued. He participated in a Durbar, an evening of literary recitations, hosted by the local Commissioner. Hafeez received an invitation and occupied a seat in the distinguished gallery. Yet, an encounter at this literary event would provide another insight into his character.

Before the proceedings began, the magistrate in charge of the event approached Hafeez and requested him to vacate his seat due to his attire. Hafeez appeared in clothing that he could afford, and it did not match the expected attire for such a dignified occasion. Hafeez paid little attention to the initial request. However, the magistrate returned a few times, insisting that Hafeez change his seat due to his attire, as it seemed unsuitable

Hafeez group photo in support of Aziz Nasl High School 1969,
Rawalpindi Pakistan.

for the occasion's dignity. This persistence reached the point where the guests sitting around Hafeez began to laugh and make jokes at his expense.

Hafeez felt deeply insulted by this ordeal. In the heat of anger, he finally responded, "The invitation was for me, not my clothes. I have come dressed in what I usually wear and what I can afford. If it was necessary for me to appear in fine clothes, the authorities should have provided me with appropriate attire along with the invitation." Hafeez continued his rebuke, "I wear this dress that I have painstakingly earned. It brings me pleasure and pride." His response left the magistrate nonplussed, and those around him now laughed at the magistrate instead.

The Deputy Commissioner, an Englishman, arrived and witnessed the situation. He warmly shook hands with Hafeez and addressed the magistrate, saying, "Don't mind it; your dress is quite suitable because your dress is not in your clothes, but in your ability and deep imagination." This incident left a deep impression on Hafeez's mind. He realized that official invitations did not necessarily equate to honor or prestige. This revelation marked another turning point in his attitude.

Hafeez's journey underscored the power of self-belief and the transformative potential of pursuing one's true passion. The narrative reveals the evolution of his character, from a novice poet with self-doubt to a confident and celebrated wordsmith. His ability to vividly capture emotions and experiences through poetry, along with his unwavering commitment to his craft, brought him recognition and respect. Most importantly, the incidents at the poetic gathering and the literary event taught him that true honor lay in one's ability and imagination, not in appearances.

Encounter with the Master: A Poet's Journey Unveiled

At this point, Hafeez found himself standing at the crossroads of uncertainty, contemplating the uncharted path into the world of poetry. The air was thick with hesitation, his gaze fixed on an elusive future that seemed both alluring and daunting. Then entered Girami, a master poet whose presence became the turning point in Hafeez's story. It was as if fate had orchestrated that encounter to breathe life into the dormant embers of creativity within him. Girami's wisdom and poetic prowess served as the catalyst, awakening a newfound passion that had lingered in the shadows of Hafeez's doubts.

As the narrative wove through these pivotal moments, it was a journey where uncertainties transformed into artistic revelations, and the flicker of inspiration evolved into a blazing trail of poetic brilliance. The stage was set, and the characters were poised for a captivating exploration of Hafeez's artistic awakening.

The setting was Jalandhar, a small-town rich in cultural heritage, where a unique story began to unfold. Here, amid the annals of literary history, the figure of Girami had shone brightly. Remarkably, Girami had never set foot in Persia, yet his mastery of the Persian language was nothing short of extraordinary. As a mosque-fellow of Hafeez's father, his presence held the promise of something extraordinary.

It all started after Hafeez's inaugural recitation, a moment that marked the beginning of a significant transformation in his life. Girami, renowned as the court poet of Nawab Sir Mahbub Ali Khan of Hyderabad, chose to retire from his illustrious courtly duties and return to his hometown, Jalandhar. While Girami's verses had the power to captivate many, it was Hafeez who particularly experienced a profound connection with his work.

Jalandhar, in its entirety, embraced Girami as a local legend, showering him with adoration. Yet, it was not just his poetry that was captivating; it was the essence of the man himself that drew Hafeez closer, much like a moth irresistibly drawn to a flame.

One day, inspired by this newfound passion, Hafeez gathered his courage and decided to send some of his own poetic creations to Girami, who had become an inspiration and an object of admiration. Anticipation mixed with uncertainty filled him as he awaited a response. Girami's reply arrived like a cherished gift. The letter was replete with corrections, suggestions, and warmth. But it was not merely guidance that Girami offered; within the folds of his letter, he expressed his eagerness to meet the budding poet in person.

The day of their meeting finally arrived, and as Hafeez entered Girami's presence, his nerves were alight with anticipation. What unfolded during their hour-long conversation transcended the boundaries of mentorship. Girami, with an astute eye for potential, discerned a spark of brilliance within Hafeez. As Hafeez left that transformative meeting, he carried with him not just valuable advice but also a profound sense of encouragement, which would sustain him through the years to come.

However, Girami's envisioned path was not without its obstacles. Hafeez's father, a man of different aspirations, looked back at his son's earlier life with disapproval. In his eyes, Hafeez's past was marked by idleness and waste, qualities far from the standards he held dear. In a candid moment, he branded Hafeez as a "base coin" within the family, implying a lack of discernible talent or purpose.

Girami, the mentor, perceived Hafeez's potential beyond these initial judgments. He envisioned the transformation of Hafeez, the "bad coin," into a "precious coin," a source of pride not only for their family but for the entire nation. With this vision firmly in mind, Girami took Hafeez under his wing, becoming not only a mentor but a guide who enriched Hafeez's understanding of the intricate nuances of Persian poetry.

As time went on, a significant transition rocked Hafeez's life. His father entrusted the family business to Hafeez's elder brother, but this decision proved unfortunate. Contracts remained unfulfilled, leading to the family's primary source of income collapsing. Hafeez's heart ached for his father's burdens, and the weight of responsibility grew heavier.

Amidst these mounting obligations, Hafeez's dedication to his literary pursuits only intensified. He immersed himself in meetings and poetry gatherings, sharing his work with the public, evolving into a notable poet. As his popularity soared, aspiring poets sought his guidance, and Hafeez found himself stepping into the role of an honorary tutor.

Amid these friendly rivalries with fellow poets, Girami again offered his wisdom. He recognized Hafeez's stature as both mentor and poet and urged him to break free from the rigid constraints of ancient poetic rules. Instead, he encouraged Hafeez to pour "new wine into old glasses," embracing innovation and originality.

These words echoed deeply within Hafeez, prompting him to refocus his efforts on his creative pursuits. However, the path was not without its sacrifices. Hafeez's heart belonged to verses, not business. This choice came at a cost; he lost business opportunities, and financial troubles were looming on the horizon.

In a reluctant move to support his family, Hafeez faced a bitter decision—selling one of the three properties inherited from his adoptive father. It was a choice that did not sit well with his father, who took immense pride in the family property, regardless of its condition; Hafeez's snobbish acquaintances echoed this sentiment. To them, the sale of property symbolized a perceived decline in his family's fortunes.

With some of the money from the property sale, Hafeez embarked on a new venture. He opened a shop in the city, crafting and selling traditional Indian caps. Yet, business acumen, which came naturally to others, eluded him. The shop faltered, leading to significant financial losses.

During these turbulent times, Hafeez and his wife were blessed with the arrival of their first child, a daughter. Fatherhood brought moments of joy, yet Hafeez's spirit remained unsettled and restless. His journey had yet to lead him to his true calling.

Then, a twist of fate took Hafeez to a dilapidated building in the village of Takya, along the Hoshiarpur Road. Hungry and fatigued, he entered the building to find a group of five or six beggars huddled together, cloaked in shawls and blankets. These destitute individuals welcomed Hafeez with warmth and kindness.

In gratitude for their hospitality, Hafeez regaled the beggars with his poems, and they, whose lives were often harsh and joyless, found themselves captivated by his verses and humor. To them, Hafeez was nothing less than a divine gift, a source of entertainment and delight. They believed that his arrival was more than mere chance; it was destiny.

Persuaded by their appeals, Hafeez agreed to stay with the beggars, taking on the role of a singing vagabond poet. This decision, although unconventional, filled him with a unique sense of fulfillment and contentment. For over three months, he became an integral part of their harmonious brotherhood.

However, as the days passed, Hafeez's conscience began to weigh heavily on his mind. He could not ignore the needs of

Hafeez Director General of Village Aid-Layla Musa center.

his family, including his wife and children. Reluctantly, he bid farewell to the beggars, who had embraced him as one of their own. Their lives, enriched by their brief union with Hafeez, were forever marked by his presence.

Hafeez's journey continued, navigating through various jobs and positions. He endured a persistent sense of disquiet, a yearning to discover his true purpose and embrace the destiny he knew was his own.

In this intricate narrative of transformation and self-discovery, the influence of Girami, the master, remained paramount. Their fateful meeting set Hafeez's poetic journey on a trajectory that would eventually lead him to the fulfillment of his deepest desires.

Hafeez's unwavering commitment to his literary passion, despite life's formidable challenges, stood as a testament to the enduring power of artistic dedication and the indelible mark of a mentor's wisdom and guidance. His journey, marked by financial troubles, personal sacrifices, and unique encounters, was a testament to the indomitable spirit of a poet who yearned to share his verses with the world.

Hafeez Jalandhari: Echoes of Empathy and Expression in British-Occupied India

Hafeez Jalandhari's life journey was characterized by his unwavering dedication to his craft and deep empathy for the oppressed, which he channeled through his poetry. In 1919, he received an invitation to attend the Punjab Congress Provincial Conference in Jalandhar, extended by Dr. S.D. Kitchlew, a seasoned Congressite. This event marked a significant turning point in his career as a poet, as he was requested to compose a poem condemning the controversial British legislation, known as the Rowllat Act. This act allowed for internment without trial and non-jury trials in specific political cases.

Despite not considering himself a political figure, Hafeez willingly offered his poetic talents to the cause. His poem, centered on the suffering and hardships faced by the impoverished in India, left an indelible impact on the audience. They cheered fervently as he recited, hoisting him on their shoulders in a moment of triumph.

Importantly, Hafeez became the first poet to dare to recite from a political platform during those turbulent times, a courageous act that would result in him being shadowed by a detective.

His bold step set the stage for other poets to follow suit, using their poetry as a means of political expression.

Following this politically charged meeting, Hafeez accepted a position as a sales manager with Singer's Sewing Machines in the Montgomery District, far from his hometown. During this time, he composed poems about the downfall of the Turks and the Great War's impact on their country. These works adhered to traditional poetic styles. Hafeez, however, yearned to express his own feelings in his unique style, blending idealism, realism, and romance into his poetry.

In his quest for a livelihood, Hafeez embarked on a year-long journey on horseback to collect installment payments for sewing machines sold on a hire-purchase system. The toil and monotony of this endeavor left him disenchanted, and he pondered the distinction between himself and the horse he rode.

Despite facing financial difficulties and various challenges, Hafeez's determination to contribute to literature remained unwavering, however. With the sale of a second family property, he ventured into starting a monthly Urdu magazine called Ejaz, meaning "miracle" in Urdu. Encouraged by Girami and other writers, he aimed to maintain a high standard for the magazine. Unfortunately, the contributions received did not meet his expectations, leading to the magazine's failure and exacerbating his financial struggles.

Amidst these trials, a dispute with his father erupted when he sold his last house. Bound by a promise of secrecy, Hafeez couldn't reveal the true reason for the sale. This secrecy infuriated his father, culminating in an unpleasant confrontation, and Hafeez was instructed to leave the city with his wife and family.

In a state of defeat, Hafeez sought refuge in Lahore. After leaving his family at his in-laws in Lahore, his wanderlust drew him to Kashmir on foot, leaving behind his worldly possessions. In the serene beauty of Kashmir, he found solace and peace for the first time in his adult life, staying for three months before returning to his family and responsibilities.

His connection with nature during this time left a deep impression on his soul. Hafeez's life, marked by resilience and a commitment to his craft, was a testament to his unyielding spirit, and his poetry continued to evolve in response to the changing world around him.

Embracing Lahore's Literary Circle: The Enchanted Evening of Poetic Reverie

After the poet's return from the solitude of Kashmir, he found himself in the heart of the bustling city of Lahore, Pakistan. There Hafeez embarked on a journey that would forever alter the course of his literary destiny. His curiosity led him to an institute where luminaries of literature, poets, and scholars of every stripe gathered. Their collective mission was to nourish Urdu literature, a realm that was still unfamiliar to Hafeez, a newcomer in Lahore.

As the evening unfolded, the room came alive with poetic recitations, each verse a melody that painted stories with words. Hafeez, too, harbored a desire to share his own creations, but the grip of shyness held him back. In this assembly of intellectuals, each individual bore titles and degrees of great significance, a stark contrast to his humble anonymity. Thus, he contented himself with a mere ticket and a secluded corner amongst the audience.

But fate had a different plan. Among the attendees were four students from Jalandhar, scholars of the university, who noticed Hafeez's presence. With enthusiasm in their eyes, they approached the secretary of the gathering, highlighting the hidden gem of a poet tucked away in the corner. Their praises painted Hafeez's talents in vibrant hues, unbeknownst to him, as he remained engrossed in the ongoing recitations.

Then, like a bolt from the blue, Hafeez heard his name called out. Bewildered and unprepared, he ascended the platform, facing a sea of learned faces. In that moment, shyness gave way to the resounding voice of his poetry, surprising everyone in attendance. Applause echoed, and the President of the gathering, Khan Bahadur, now the esteemed Sir Abdul Qadir, extended his congratulations to Hafeez. In that brief encounter, Hafeez's journey into the literary circles of Lahore was irrevocably sealed.

Thus, Hafeez emerged as a shining poet, a rising sun on the vast horizon of Urdu literature. Khan Bahadur's words held the promise of a fruitful friendship and mutual respect that would flourish over the years, forever altering the trajectory of Hafeez's life.

Hafeez, the People's Poet 1964.

V

Life's Journey

5

Personal and Professional Struggles

Hafeez's life unfolded into a new chapter, thrusting him into the realm of professional journalism. A golden opportunity materialized as a job offer from a Lahore-based magazine, promising a monthly remuneration of sixty rupees—a beacon of hope amid financial difficulties, eagerly accepted by Hafeez.

Yet, this journalistic journey was marred by the whims of an eccentric proprietor. As the day for Hafeez's wages approached, the owner conveniently vanished, his memory selectively forgetful when it came to paying his employee. The first month passed without salary, and Hafeez's reserved nature prevented confrontation. Optimism clung to the belief that two months' wages would arrive in the next cycle, but history repeated itself, month after month, as Hafeez's debts grew. The breaking point came when he mustered the courage to request payment, receiving only a fraction of what was owed.

Financial distress intensified with peculiar tasks assigned by the magazine. Hafeez found himself correcting and composing articles and poems submitted by aspiring but questionable writers. Additionally, unscrupulous individuals paid the proprietor to publish their work under their names, tasks Hafeez undertook as a ghost-writer, creating extraordinary pieces that went uncredited.

These challenging days, coupled with irregular salary payments, tested Hafeez. Yet, driven by responsibilities to his family and the support of his mother and sisters in Jalandhar, he persevered. Amidst exploitation, his passion for writing remained undaunted, finding solace in the creation of children's stories during late-night hours.

From Poet to Chief Editor to the People's Poet: Navigating the Worlds of Creativity and Journalism

After eighteen months of service, Hafeez seized a promising opportunity as the chief editor of two esteemed magazines, *Hazar Dastan* and *Naunihal.* Regular salary brought relief, but a dispute led to his resignation, propelling him into positions at *Tahzib-i-Niswan* and *Phul.*

Transitioning, Hafeez's reputation as a writer soared. Carving a niche with a unique poetic style, he departed from conventional romanticism, injecting pathos, and realism into his verses. His commitment to Urdu poetry faced challenges from jealous peers, but he remained above the fray, guided by luminaries, like Dr. Sir Mohammed Iqbal and Sir Abdul Qadir. His association with influential figures, notably Pandit Hari Chand Akhtar, bolstered his fame beyond Punjab's borders.

Despite facing trials, Hafeez's journey symbolized talent emerging from unexpected places, resilience, and determination. From overcoming shyness to gaining recognition, navigating financial challenges, and combating exploitation, his enduring strength in familial responsibility and creativity shone brightly. As both a chief editor and a unique poet, he exemplified the enduring impact of individuality, overcoming obstacles in the pursuit of his calling. His journey transcended boundaries, leaving a remarkable impression on Urdu literature.

From Courtly Verse to Disillusioned Rhyme: Court Poet Hafeez's Transition

In the annals of 1925, a pivotal chapter unfolded as Hafeez ascended to the esteemed position of Durbar (Court) Poet for His Highness the Mir of Khairpur (Sind). The promise of financial relief and fame held hope, intertwining with his fervent dedication to poetry. Yet, the elation of this appointment was swiftly eclipsed by tragedy, as eleven days into his tenure, the somber toll of his mother's passing cast a pall over his new-found responsibilities.

Amid the opulent revelry of the court, Hafeez found himself ensnared in the suffocating grip of grief, unable to partake in the superficial joys that surrounded him. The dream of bringing

Visiting Rangoon 1957.

honor and joy to his mother through his newfound acclaim shattered under the weight of sorrow. Desperate for solace and closure, he sought leave to pay his final respects, only to be met with callous indifference and disdain from courtiers whose hearts remained untouched by empathy.

In the hallowed halls of Khairpur, amidst the murmurs of sycophancy and the clinking of golden goblets, Hafeez retreated into the depths of his sorrow, finding solace in the verses that flowed from his anguished soul. It was here, amidst the shadows of opulence and deceit, that the seeds of "Raqqasah" were sown, a lyrical masterpiece born from the crucible of pain and disillusionment, critiquing the moral compromise festering at the heart of courtly life.

With each stanza meticulously-crafted, Hafeez poured his grief, his anger, and his unyielding spirit into his poetic creation, refusing to compromise his artistic integrity for the sake of fleeting favor or hollow praise. Yet, as the echoes of his recital reverberated through the marble halls, his words, pregnant with truth and defiance, drew the ire of those whose power rested upon the perpetuation of falsehoods.

His dismissal from the court was swift, a harsh rebuke for daring to challenge the status quo, yet Hafeez stood undaunted, his spirit unbroken by the shackles of oppression. Refusing to bow before the whims of tyrants or the demands of hypocrites, he embraced this as a badge of honor, a testament to his unwavering commitment to truth and artistic expression.

Upon regaining his freedom, the Poet Laureate returned to the humble confines of his home, his heart heavy with the weight of disappointment yet buoyed by the knowledge that he had remained true to himself amidst the tempest of adversity. This tumultuous chapter in his life marked a turning point, solidifying Hafeez's commitment to truth and artistic expression, regardless of the cost or the consequences.

As the echoes of "Raqqasah" lingered in the air, resonating with the hearts of those who dared to listen, Hafeez emerged from the crucible of his trials, transformed, yet unbroken, his spirit tempered by the fires of adversity, his resolve steeled against the winds of compromise. And though his path may have been fraught with peril and uncertainty, he strode forward with his head held high, a beacon of light amidst the encroaching darkness, a testament to the enduring power of the human spirit to triumph over adversity and injustice.

VI

Achievements and Recognition

6

Breakthroughs and Milestones

Naghma Zar-Garden of Melodies:
A Poet's Harmony

Upon his poignant return to Lahore, Hafeez paid a heartfelt visit to his mother's hallowed resting place—a moment teeming with profound emotion. He stood amidst the silent gravestones, the weight of his past and the call of his poetic future intertwined in a heart-wrenching symphony.

A sense of melancholy washed over him, feeling somewhat adrift in the sea of life's complexities. In the shadows of that sacred ground, he temporarily shelved his poetic endeavors, allowing the intricate tapestry of existence to simmer in the background, like the secrets of the universe waiting to be unveiled.

Four months later, fate unfurled its enigmatic banner. Sir Abdul Qadir, Punjab's Minister of Education, orchestrated an extravagant All-India "Mushairah" in Shimla. Hafeez, the rising star of poetry, was summoned to partake in this literary extravaganza—a celestial assembly of luminaries, including political heavyweights, government officials, revered writers, and intellectuals.

As the journey to Shimla unfolded, it transformed into an exuberant escapade, where the aromatic brew of tea flowed ceaselessly, and culinary inhibitions were gleefully discarded by the ensemble of poets. However, the indulgence in this culinary revelry took an unexpected toll on Hafeez's vocal cords, leaving him temporarily bereft of his most precious instrument—his voice.

Sir Abdul Qadir, amused by the peculiar cause of Hafeez's vocal malady, was unwavering in his resolve to ensure the poet's participation. "You are the luminary of our spectacle," he chortled, "yet you find yourself ensnared in a vocal quagmire." Medical aid was hastily summoned, offering a semblance of relief, yet full recovery remained elusive as uncertainty loomed over Hafeez's poetic contribution.

As the poetic symposium commenced, Hafeez was called upon to recite his verses. Initially hesitant, due to the fragility of his vocal cords, the audience's resolute insistence could not be silenced. With sheer determination, Hafeez summoned every ounce of his willpower to rally his voice, which, despite its huskiness, erupted like a mesmerizing poetic tempest.

Each couplet he uttered became a thunderclap of emotion, met with roaring applause and impassioned pleas for an encore.

The ambiance mirrored the electrifying fervor of a captivating concert's encore, each word a flame setting the hearts of the audience ablaze.

His voice, once lost, gradually regained its former vigor, infused with newfound vitality, breathing life into the poetic realm. Although his throat remained hoarse, Hafeez couldn't resist gracing the audience with more than a dozen of his most cherished poems. This electrifying performance catapulted him to the pinnacle of that day's poetic hierarchy—an undisputed maestro, whose fame as a poetic genius radiated like the first rays of a rising sun, illuminating the literary horizon with unparalleled brilliance.

The public's insatiable hunger for Hafeez's verses in printed form was undeniable. Driven by an unquenchable desire to see his poetry in tangible print, Hafeez, undeterred by financial obstacles, made the ultimate sacrifice. He mortgaged cherished possessions to secure the necessary funds and, in 1925, triumphantly published his first book, "*Naghma Zar*" (*Garden of Melodies*).

The book garnered widespread acclaim, particularly from progressive writers. Girami, overwhelmed by Hafeez's verses, penned a heartfelt ode in appreciation, which found its rightful place within the pages of the book. Leading newspapers and journals hailed Hafeez's book with effusive praise, heralding it as a literary marvel that had ignited the passions of the reading world.

Yet, within the ranks of poets belonging to the old school of thought, the reception was tainted by personal bias, casting shadows over Hafeez's revolutionary artistry. The clash of tradition and innovation ignited fierce debates, where hearts and minds were battlegrounds, and the verdict remained contentious.

In a world divided by tradition and innovation, Hafeez carved a niche for himself. Every stroke of his pen was a poetic revelation, and every word was a testament to the extraordinary. His name became a beacon, drawing seekers of beauty and wisdom to the *Garden of Melodies*, where the drama of life and poetry forever intertwined.

Footlights to Fame and New Horizons

Hafeez's journey from 1925 to 1927 opened doors to influential figures who left an indelible mark on his path. Among them were Nawab Masud Jang and Nawab Sardar Yar Jang Bahadur, remarkable individuals from Hyderabad, with whom deep and lasting bonds formed.

In profound conversations with Nawab Masud Jang, grandson of Sir Syed Ahmed Khan, Hafeez delved into the essence of art and the responsibilities of a poet. Nawab Sardar Yar Jang Bahadur, chief of the religious department and a notable writer, shared Hafeez's passion for preserving and promoting Urdu literature. Their camaraderie was built on a shared vision for Urdu literature to flourish and inspire generations.

As Hafeez immersed himself in these friendships, the sights and sounds of Hyderabad came alive. The bustling streets, fragrant bazaars, and echoes of poetic verses in grand havelis shaped Hafeez's poetic journey. Amid sensory experiences, he was invited to an "At Home symposium" hosted by Nawab

Fakhr Yar Jang Bahadur, attended by Prime Minister Maharajah Sir Kishan Parshad. Hafeez's recitations left a profound impact, with thunderous applause and awe in the eyes of the audience.

One evening, bathed in the soft glow of the moon, Hafeez recited his poetry exclusively for a select gathering at Strachey Hall. The atmosphere charged with anticipation, Hafeez delivered distinctive, realistic, and thought-provoking poetry. His words resonated deeply, leaving the audience in awe. The evening marked a decisive defeat for the old school of poetry, and the appreciation received was etched in his heart—a testament to the power of authentic and impactful poetry.

After his electrifying performance at Strachey Hall, he reflected under the starry sky. Personal revelations played a pivotal role in Hafeez's journey. The weight of a newfound fame and responsibility stirred a whirlwind of emotions. In this moment, he remembered his humble beginnings and teachers who nurtured his love for poetry. Dedicated to preserving Urdu literature, Hafeez's legacy marked contributions to education.

As his journey unfolded, the influence on All India Mushaira became evident. In 1928, excluded initially, Hafeez's attendance marked a pivotal moment. Breaking free from old customs, he delivered a stirring poem on "The Poet's Aim," leaving a lasting impression. The night was a symphony of emotions, from awe to inspiration, hinting at greater heights in Hafeez's poetic journey.

It is noteworthy that context and historical background set the stage for the various unfolding events. Hyderabad's rich

-A memorable poetic gathering. Hafeez reciting surrounded by - Ustadi Azhar - Hafeez Ho Lia Uri -Zia Pashgiri team and Ghana amongt women.

cultural heritage and patronage of the arts played a significant role. Hafeez rose to prominence, leaving a lasting impact on Urdu literature. His legacy became one of artistic integrity, commitment to principles, and a unique poetic style challenging traditional norms.

Master of Epics: Shahnama-i-Islam Volume 1

The year 1928 stands as a landmark in the poet's career. In that year, Hafeez started the chief work of his life, Shahnama-i-Islam. His journey began in a modest house with a tiny room, facing grimy and malodorous surroundings.

Despite the nauseating environment, Hafeez honed his craft, forging his path to recognition as the Firdausi of his era. He dared to bridge the chasm between history and poetry, conceiving the audacious idea of Shahnama-i-Islam—an epic narrative chronicling the heroic exploits of Islam's great figures and the life of Prophet Muhammad.

This audacious undertaking set him apart, challenging norms of thirteen centuries of Islamic history. Balancing multiple roles, Hafeez faced a daunting choice. He relinquished work from publishing houses to devote time to his opus, sacrificing financial stability. His unwavering faith and belief in a brighter future fueled his determination.

In 1928, Hafeez introduced his unique style, breaking free from old customs. Esteemed critics acknowledged him as an inventor and creator. The influence sparked a new generation of poets who, captivated by Hafeez's style, followed in his footsteps. Hafeez's journey, marked by skepticism and support, emphasizes the resilience needed to turn vision into reality.

In 1929, an invitation arrived that would elevate Hafeez's reputation. He attended an At-Home symposium event in Shimla, hosted by Captain Malik Mumtaz Mohammad Tiwana. During the event, the host admired Hafeez for his poetic achievements, offering a generous sum for a copy of his book, Shahnama-i-Islam; this unexpected support deepened Hafeez's sense of achievement, alleviating financial burdens.

However, Hafeez's journey to Quetta and Lahore, contributing to a children's weekly publication, took a shocking turn. His beloved daughter tragically had slipped and fallen into a well, while fetching water, leading to her demise. This profound loss shook Hafeez to the core, affecting his emotional well-being and health.

Leaving Jalandhar and upon arriving in Lahore, Hafeez discovered Model Town, intending to secure a rental home. Faced with unavailability, he opted to construct his own house. However, unfulfilled promises by the Model Town Society led to unrest. Frustrated, Hafeez initiated the publication of "Karzar" to shed light on the issues, leading to a legal battle he ultimately won.

Soz O Saz (Flame and Music)

In the same year, Hafeez introduced his second collection of literary pieces and poems, "Soz-O-Saz 1925-1933." Esteemed critics acknowledged Hafeez as an inventor and creator, paying him well-deserved tributes. His influence on Urdu literature manifested in magazines and poetic symposiums, inspiring a new generation of poets.

His collection entitled "Flame and Music" contains all songs, romantic and natural, composed by him between the years of 1925 and 1933. The preface to the collection was written by Pandit Hari Chand Akhtar, M.A., in which he summed up the contributions of the poet.

> The author of *Shahnama-i-Islam* and *Naghmazar* no longer stands in need of the services of an experienced and long-winded usher to cry ..oyez- oyez.. before him to announce his arrival. It is no doubt one of the well-established and accepted conventions of civilized society that a new arrival and a stranger has to be introduced to those present, therefore, when Hafeez as a poet first arrived, the ritual of introduction was duly performed in **1925**.

When *Naghma Zar*, the first collection of his poems, was published, some appreciative introductory verses were written by the late poet laureate Maulana Girami. Professor A. S Bokhari Petras also paid homage by way of a preface. The work and style of a poet can be judged from the appreciation he gets in his own times, and the promise which he shows at finding a permanent place in the gallery of poetic artists.

From **1928** onwards, since Hafeez began to depict natural scenery and to give an expression to his sentiments in the small musical meters, giving a local colour to rhythm and rhyme, you are sure to find in any Urdu magazine that you may pick up, and in any poetical symposium that you may attend, quiet a number of poets following in the footsteps of Hafeez. The majority of those who try to imitate Hafeez, not being endowed with natural aptitude, fail miserably, and make themselves a laughingstock of the discerning and critical public; but here we are not concerned with the fact whether the limitation is a success or a failure.

But if limitation is really the best way of appreciation, then it cannot be denied that the new style of Hafeez enjoys the undisputed position of being the pioneer and has acquired for itself a permanent and prominent place in Urdu literature. On the one hand learned and eminent critics find themselves compelled to award Hafeez the tribute due to an inventor and a creator, and on the other hand the contemporary poetic luminaries have been carried off their feet by the new whirlwind. Even those pillars of conservatism who, for reasons best known to themselves, used to cry down Hafeez's inventions, are now imitating him for the sake of their existence in the world of literature.

In 1935-1937, Hafeez's journey reflects an unwavering dedication to literary greatness despite adversity. In creating Shahnama-i-Islam, he sacrificed financial stability, showcasing idealism and faith. Overcoming skepticism, public support marked his transformation from adversity to the people's poet, highlighting the enduring spirit of dedication in artistic pursuit.

"Poet's Pilgrimage" transports us to the year 1935 when the revered poet, Abul Asar Hafeez Jalandhari, embarked on a sacred journey to Mecca and Medina, a lifelong dream fulfilled through the gracious invitation of the Nawab of Bahawalpur. This pilgrimage was more than a mere voyage; it was a divine gift, one that Hafeez had yearned for since 1926 when he penned a heartfelt devotional tribute, titled "Salam" to the Holy Land. The Nawab's invitation felt like an answered prayer, and it marked the beginning of a transformative odyssey.

At the quayside in Karachi, there were many of the poet's admirers to see him off. They all shared their joy in his taking this sacred journey to the holy land. The congregation requested the Nawab of Bahawalpur to ask Hafeez to recite his famous poem, "Meera Salaam Lega." Hafeez was deeply moved by this request. From the deck of the ship, *Rahmani,* Hafeez recited his poem to an audience on the quayside full of many of his true and sincere admirers.

The atmosphere was dramatic, with the ship in the background, the poet on the deck, eyes full of tears, and his voice shaking with emotion for all those there, many seeing him as the true spokesman of their own inner feelings. As he recited "Mera Salaam Leja," the sincerity and the reverent note of his poem seemed to affect even the tender emotions of nature; for these ten minutes, even the crude song of the seagulls stopped. This was one of the most dramatic and cherished moments that had ever been carved into the poet's memory.

The heartfelt recitation earned Hafeez thunderous applause and shouts of "Hafeez Zindabad" (Long live Hafeez) from the grateful onlookers. This emotional send-off, coupled with Hafeez's fervent desire to visit the holy land, infused his pilgrimage with joy and purpose.

Hafeez's journey took him to Medina, a city that stirred his soul. Here, he composed another "Salaam" to personally pay homage to the Holy Prophet. His melodious voice filled the tranquil air as he offered his *Salaam*, and in that sacred moment, Hafeez felt enriched by a unique sense of composure and inner peace, as if he had somehow already visited these holy places in his being.

Medina allowed Hafeez to connect with Indian settlers who had established themselves there. However, it also introduced him to a peculiar situation. The Arabian public labeled him as an imposter and described a "real Hafeez" with a long, traditional beard, seemingly from a medieval era. Hafeez, with his sense of humor intact, took this misrepresentation in stride. Later, when he met the impersonator, the explanation was simple – he had impersonated Hafeez for financial gain, believing Hafeez wouldn't mind.

Mohammed Ali Jinnah (left), Liaqat Ali Khan (center),
Poet Hafeez Jalandhari (far right)

Throughout his stay in Medina, Hafeez actively participated in meetings and charitable endeavors. At one gathering, he initiated a collection for the orphans of Medina. After twenty-one days in this sacred city, Hafeez embarked on the journey to Mecca, where he fulfilled his religious obligation of performing Haj.

In Mecca, Hafeez had the privilege of meeting His Majesty Jalalatul-Mulk Sultan Ibn-i-Saud, to whom he presented his magnum opus, the Shahnama. The poet lingered in Mecca for twenty days, and as the time for departure approached, he found it agonizing to leave the land that felt like home. Hafeez had previously written about Mecca in his Shahnama, and his imagination had so vividly captured the essence of these holy places, that it felt like a spiritual homecoming. After forty-one days of solitude and serenity, Hafeez reluctantly returned home, where a plethora of responsibilities awaited him.

Tragedy had once again struck Hafeez's family with the passing of his brothers, leaving behind widows and children who became his moral obligation to support. This additional burden weighed heavily on his shoulders, leading him to resume his duties upon returning.

Despite the personal grief and responsibilities he bore, Hafeez continued to find solace in his poetry, singing with ecstatic love as the ultimate expression of the human spirit. His poignant composition, "The Soul," even found recognition and was translated by the celebrated Bengali musician, Mr. Dilip Kumar Roy.

"Poet's Pilgrimage" is a testament to the profound significance of Hafeez Jalandhari's 1935 journey, capturing the essence of his spiritual odyssey, emotional encounters, and the enduring power of his poetry in his life.

In 1936, Hafeez Jalandhari, the celebrated poet, received a prestigious honor that would forever mark this year in the history of Urdu literature. The Nawab of Tonk extended an invitation to Hafeez, recognizing his exceptional literary contributions. As a State Guest in the Nawab's court, Hafeez was bestowed with the prestigious titles of "Malikushshoara" (the Poet-Laureate) and "Hassanulmulk Bahadur" (the Prince of Poets), serving as a testament to his literary eminence and a celebration of his art.

Upon his return home, Hafeez was met with a unanimous resolution from the scholars and literary figures of Jalandhar, expressing gratitude to the Nawab of Tonk for his patronage and for honoring their beloved luminary. Notably, Hafeez had already received the title of "Khan Sahib" from the government in 1934, further solidifying his position.

In the beginning of 1937, Hafeez suffered a great deal from whitlow on his right thumb, necessitating an urgent operation. The operation resulted in disfiguring his thumb. Because of this, his work began to suffer seriously. For nearly ten months, Hafeez endured this very painful trouble. At one point even amputating the arm was considered. Fortunately, a Hakim, a doctor specializing in alternative medicine, arrived on the scene in time and opposed the amputation, recommending an ointment instead, which slowly helped the poet to recover.

Hafeez was convalescing, one very noble friend of the poet called him to Delhi, which forced him out of his sick bed. On his arrival in Delhi, this friend dosed him with aspirins and told him that he had promised the public a recitation. Hafeez fainted from sheer fatigue and weakness after an hour and a half.

Soon after Hafeez was invited by some friends to join them in Kashmir to recuperate. However, once more he was forced to attend meetings and was dragged to the mushairas. Instead of getting the relief he needed, he was paying heavily for the price of popularity. His arm in a sling was still painful but the Kashmir public insatiably demanded his recitations for long and tiring hours.

However, Kashmir was a muse for the poet. He embodied his great appreciation for its beauty in a poem, which, subsequently, appeared in a book form under the title *Taswir-i-Kashmir,* "The

Picture of Kashmir". This very powerful and descriptive poem, in which the poet has, with great art and ingenuity, contrasted the poverty and squalor of the men of Kashmir with the superb grandeur of its natural beauty.

He recited *Taswir-i-Kashmir* twice at a grand poetic symposium. In writing this poem there was another thought in the poet's mind, expressing his wish for a strong unity between Hindus and the Muslims. The poet's vision can be noted in dedications to Sheikh Mohammad Abdulla, and Pandit Pren Nath Bazaz.

Hafeez's idealism was described by the great literary critic, Sir Ross Masud, who wrote in his introduction. The following are a few lines which read:

> "My Hafeez is neither a preacher nor a political pro-pagandist. He neither meddles with politics nor does he sermonize. I love Hafeez's style. His simple and effective poetry produces in me a feeling in which I get entirely lost but cannot exactly describe in words. Whenever I read him, I am convinced that of all the notable Urdu poets whom I know, he is the only one about whom I can say with confidence that he in his field of work confines himself to the interpretation of what he sees and feels, and in this field, none equals him. Hafeez's heart is like a palace of mirrors."

Sir Ross Masud eloquently delves into Hafeez's verses, meticulously unraveling the vibrant tapestry of contemporary life that traversed the poet's mind. Yet, Hafeez was not merely an ordinary poet; he emerged as a maestro of reflection and emotions. Within the palace of his heart, where joy and sorrow, good and bad, gracefully danced, Hafeez's verses eloquently narrated their stories.

With a palette of vivid and evocative expressions, Hafeez's poetry had the transformative power to elicit smiles, frowns, pride, and moments of profound contemplation. His verses opened the doors to a palace of mirrors, an intimate reflection of human existence, a sanctuary of emotions where readers could immerse themselves.

Hafeez, in his poetic brilliance, allowed the world to explore this rich tapestry, offering laughter, deep sighs, tears, and sometimes even prompting screams for rescue. In the hands of Hafeez, poetry became a dynamic journey through the spectrum of human experience.

Echoes of Solace: Hafeez's Sojourn in England and the Unspoken Connection with Anela

In the luminous ascent of Hafeez's literary eminence, accolades cascaded from every corner of India. By 1947, even the discerning gaze of His Exalted Highness the Nizam's Government acknowledged the profound worth of Hafeez's magnum opus, Shahnama-i-Islam. A monthly allowance of three hundred rupees for three years was granted, a testament to the poet's undeniable influence.

Despite this success, the trials of the past year and the financial burden Hafeez carried led to a nervous breakdown. Advised by a doctor and encouraged by Sir Abdul Qadir, he embarked on a journey to Europe, seeking respite from his demanding admirers. His destination was to England, where he arrived in February 1938 and found solace among old friends, despite the language barrier.

Intending to rest, Hafeez encountered little reprieve. In the first two months, various Indian organizations arranged meetings in his honor, expressing delight in having the revered poet in England. On April 9, the Muslim Society of Great Britain organized a reception at Eccleston Square, S.W.1.

The weekly *Muslim Gazette of London* reported:

> The guests, who had started pouring in at 4 p.m., had reached such an unprecedented number by the time fixed, that the officers of the society began to find great difficulty arranging and accommodating the crowd in the limited space at their disposal. This underscored Hafeez's popularity in England. Many English Muslims, unable to comprehend the poet's language, were nevertheless enchanted by his sweet and melodious voice. Since the death of Dr. Sir Mohammad Iqbal, Hafeez Abul Asar Jalandhari is regarded the leading Urdu poet of India to-day.
>
> *This appeared on the 2nd of July 1938*
> *in The Times of India, Bombay.*

During Easter, Hafeez was invited to Glasgow for the launch of the ship, *El Hind.* The poem he had written for the occasion resonated amid cheers. The National League for Empire Friendship had Hafeez recite at a luncheon, and the weekly *Great Britain and the East* reported, 'He impressed the audience greatly by his poems.'

Poet Hafeez Jalandhari surrounded by guests, dignitaries and supporters, England

The Home Press was as intrigued by Hafeez's work abroad as was the foreign press in reporting his movements. The *Times of India, Bombay*, published accounts of his activities in England on the 2nd of July 1938.

'The President and members of the Hindustani Union were at-home to visitors from India. The most interesting feature of the proceedings was the reading of three Urdu poems, composed in London by Abul Asar Hafeez Jalandhari, one of the most sought-after persons in the Indian Colony.'

Amidst this whirlwind, a chance encounter brought Anela, a young woman of Lithuanian descent, into Hafeez's orbit. Drawn by the haunting beauty of his poem 'Jaag Soz-i-Ishq Jaag,' Anela, a newcomer to Urdu poetry, found herself captivated. Invited to a gathering, she hesitated, yearning for a more intimate introduction to the poet.

This introduction happened in a humble setting, while teaching English to a young Indian boy, where she met the poet when he came to visit the family. She eventually found herself intertwined with the poet's life, taking on the task of tutoring him in English herself.

Anela's subsequent interactions with Hafeez unveiled the layers of his personality—a man burdened by life's adversities, yet a beacon of poetic brilliance. The enchantment of his recitations, especially 'Jaag Soz-i-Ishq Jaag,' transcended language barriers, imprinting itself on Anela's memory.

As Hafeez's schedule in England unfolded, so did the challenges he faced. Meetings, luncheons, teas, and dinners became the fabric of his days, with the demand for his poetry ever-increasing. The toll on Hafeez became apparent as fatigue set in, leaving him yearning for respite. Despite his longing for rest, his commitment to studying, writing the third volume of the Shahnama, and learning English left him with little reprieve.

Anela, serving as Hafeez's English tutor, witnessed his struggle with the language barrier. His halting English and exhaustion painted a poignant picture of a man caught in the throes of public admiration. Hafeez's sincerity in wanting to connect with English society, coupled with his unwavering dedication to his craft, earned Anela's admiration.

However, another surprise awaited when Anela discovered Hafeez, after an evening recital, in a precarious state. Fainting and ailing, he was escorted home by Sir Abdul Qadir. Overwhelmed by ceaseless recitals and meetings, Hafeez decided to "cry halt" and sought refuge from the public gaze. He retreated to a bungalow in Jaywick, Clacton-on-Sea, finding solace in the refreshing isolation of the seaside resort. Here, inspired by the tranquil surroundings, he completed the first thousand verses of the third volume of Shahnama-i-Islam.

Returning to London, Hafeez maintained a low profile, shielded by the anonymity of his whereabouts. Anela, in her own small way, contributed to this respite.

Meanwhile, Hafeez's contemplations on the plight of women in India emerged. Advocating for their intrinsic value, he viewed women as the architects of the nation's future.

In conversations about Hafeez's own gender, Anela was taken aback by his vehement critique of men who, according to him, plucked the metaphorical flowers (women) only to discard them. Despite his intensity, Hafeez's inner sentiments revealed a profound sympathy for women.

His worldview extended beyond gender, believing in the equality of all people worldwide. His humanitarian ideals rested on the conviction that differences in nationalities and lifestyles should not divide humanity. Man, he argued, should strive to prevent, not wage war, directing efforts against the common adversary- evil.

Amidst his towering fame, Hafeez retained a natural simplicity. Shy, reserved, and untouched by the spoils of celebrity, he looked upon those less fortunate with kindness. Anela, through her intimate encounters with the poet, uncovered the layers of his personality—a man of depth, conviction, and an unyielding commitment to his craft.

In revisiting that fateful morning when Anela found Hafeez alone and ailing, a profound realization emerged. Despite the accolades and adulation, Hafeez, like any human, sought respite from the relentless demands of public life. His vulnerability laid bare, challenging the societal expectations thrust upon those who find themselves in the public eye.

One morning, there was a surprise when the audience learned that Hafeez was intending on leaving them so suddenly. It was impossible to find him in the midst of all his admirers. The room was buzzing with conversation.

After tea, the guests settled down, and Hafeez appeared and recited his newly composed poem, "The World of the West." "Afrang-ki- Dunya," in which he described his impressions of Western civilization. It was immensely enjoyed. The continuous clapping, accompanied by the shouts of "very good, wonderful, wah, wah" coming from listeners made the occasion very exciting. The spirit of this poem moved his audience deeply.

Sir Abdul Qadir later read out the translation in English, and the meeting then came to a close; but not without goodbyes, congratulations, and much photo-taking. The poet's friends expressed their desire to see him once again in England. Hafeez also expressed his intention to visit England again 'soon.' Anela felt sad about the poet's departure but felt very proud of the fact that it was she who had helped him to speak and write a little English, although teaching him a difficult task at first, as both of them were ignorant of each other's language. They found hunting up many words for the English and Urdu dictionaries quite amusing.

It was a cold English September morning on the day Hafeez left England. Sir Abdul Qadir and some other Indian gentlemen were at the station to say goodbye to him. Sir Abdul looked a little sad, for he would miss the poet's daily visits. The same signs of parting sorrow were visible on the poet's face as it was a tense moment. In a fit of distress, he said, "Now I am anxious to start."

Sir Abdul Qadir then remarked, "That is the poet's impatience in you."

Hafeez Jalandhari, a celebrated poet known for his profound contributions to Urdu literature, captivated dignitaries and garnered supporters alike during his visit to England. With his eloquent verses and insightful musings, Jalandhari enchanted audiences, drawing admiration from intellectuals, diplomats, and literary aficionados. His poetic prowess transcended cultural boundaries, fostering a deep appreciation for Urdu poetry among diverse audiences in England.

Throughout his stay, Jalandhari engaged in meaningful dialogues, sharing the rich heritage of Urdu poetry and its significance in bridging cultural divides. His interactions with dignitaries highlighted the universal appeal of his work, underscoring the power of poetry to forge connections and foster understanding.

Supporters of Jalandhari in England championed his literary legacy, organizing events and gatherings to honor his contributions to Urdu literature. Their enthusiasm and admiration reflected the profound impact of Jalandhari's poetry, inspiring a newfound appreciation for the beauty and depth of Urdu verse among English-speaking audiences.

Abul Asar Hafeez Jalandhari's magnum opus, the 'Shahna-ma-i-Islam,' is a unique account of history in verse in a three-volume epic. Hafeez crafted this narrative, that intertwined emotion and wisdom, reviving the art of storytelling in poetry and rekindling the flame of faith within.

In a world grappling with spiritual stagnation, Hafeez felt a need to awaken humanity's dormant spirits, even expressing what moved him to undertake such a monumental task in the poem itself:

> Deadness of spirit prevails over the Muslims everywhere:
> And the stillness of death enshrouds them.
> Once again, I wish to warm their blood;
> And pierce their hearts with fiery darts of poetry.
> And tell them such trilling bold stirring stories

Hafeez also made reference to his pilgrimage to the obscure tomb of Kutbuddin Aibak, the first Indian Muslim king, unknown to the thronging crowds of the city, Lahore. It fueled Hafeez's determination to give voice to what has been forgotten and lost:

> You can once again give the message of freedom to the oppressed
> You can once again make live noble deeds with your pen.
> Islam which conferred independence on the oppressed
> Islam which brought brotherhood in place of exploitation,
> Islam which bestowed kingship even on slaves
> That Islam can even today revive its noble deeds.

Hafeez's first volume encompasses the origins of Islam, from Adam's birth and Ishmael's miracles at the Zam Zam spring to Prophet Mohammed's birth and his life up until he declared himself the prophet. Hafeez described a desolate desert where this saga unfolded:

A Desert where man prefers death to life;
A Desert whose heart is the habitat of the fire-like rays of the sun;
A Desert whose sands since the beginning of time are longing to
see the face of water.
The gusts of sand storms were here in plenty,
It was a valley so full of horrors that even terror itself felt terrified.
But this valley was unique in the world.
It was one day to become the center of true religion.

The second volume symbolizes resilience against overwhelming odds. More than one thousand couplets vividly describe of the first open war waged by the Quresh of Mecca against the Holy Prophet and his followers, who had taken refuge in Medina, called the "Battle of Badar", in which the Muslims were victorious.

The third volume encompassed the Battle of Uhud, in which Muslims were defeated, a gripping narrative of human frailty and indomitable spirit in adversity, reflecting our collective struggles for righteousness.

Hafeez's three-volume narrative 'Shahnama-i-Islam' emerges as a timeless masterpiece, traversing the landscapes of Islamic history, unveiling tales of valor and sacrifice. His poetry captured the essence of faith in order to revive it as a source of strength, justice, and resilience.

Hafeez Jalandhari's life unfolds as a profound tapestry, interwoven with the threads of poetry, struggle, spirituality, and a ceaseless quest for justice. His journey from the humble streets of Jalandhar to the esteemed corridors of literary acclaim illuminates the transformative power of words and the resilience of the human spirit.

In the realm of Urdu poetry, Hafeez's legacy endures as a testament to the enduring power of literature to transcend boundaries and inspire generations. His 'Shahnama-i-Islam' stands as a monumental contribution, weaving a narrative that resonates with the collective human experience—a timeless odyssey of faith, struggle, and triumph.

Hafeez's commitment to social justice and the empowerment of the oppressed remains an indelible mark on his legacy. The poignant verses of 'Lab Pe Aati Hai Dua Ban Ke Tamanna Meri' echo through time, a melody of hope and aspiration. His advocacy for the rights of women and the downtrodden reflects a visionary spirit ahead of its time.

As a poet laureate, Hafeez's influence extended beyond the realms of literature. His recognition as "Malikushshoara" and "Hassanulmulk Bahadur" amongst various other titles, underscore the profound impact of his poetic prowess on the cultural and literary landscape of his era.

The 'Poet's Pilgrimage' in 1935 unfolds as a transformative odyssey, marking Hafeez's spiritual awakening and leaving an indelible imprint on his poetic canvas. His sojourn in England, as narrated through the lens of Anela, unveils the vulnerabilities of an artist in the public eye, seeking solace and connection amidst the demands of fame.

Hafeez's poetry, like a palace of mirrors, reflects the myriad facets of the human experience. From the ethereal beauty of Kashmir to the bustling streets of England, his verses serve as a timeless guide, prompting introspection, compassion, and a deeper understanding of the world.

The journey through the 'Shahnama-i-Islam' transcends the boundaries of time and culture, offering a narrative that resonates with the universal quest for faith, justice, and freedom. Hafeez's poetic retelling of Islamic history becomes a beacon, guiding readers through the annals of time, inspiring reflection, and contemplation.

In the mosaic of his life, Hafeez Jalandhari emerges as a champion of faith, a voice for the voiceless, and a poet laureate whose verses continue to echo through the corridors of literary history. His legacy invites readers to embark on a poetic pilgrimage, traversing the landscapes of human emotion, spirituality, and the timeless pursuit of truth.

As the pages of Hafeez's life unfold, his words endure, inviting generations to explore the palace of mirrors within their hearts, where the reflections of joy, sorrow, love, and humanity dance in eternal resonance.

The Story behind the National Anthem of Pakistan

The story behind the writing of the anthem is one of profound dedication. The canvas of creativity stretched wide as Hafeez undertook the monumental responsibility, immersing himself in a solitary cocoon for an intense three-month period.

Within the sanctuary of his isolation, the poet delved into the profound depths of his creative well, each line meticulously crafted with unwavering devotion. His seclusion transformed into a crucible, a testament to the profound commitment he harbored to bestow justice upon this monumental task.

Through those solitary months, Hafeez toiled with diligence, transcending the mere selection of words to an artful weighing of each one. Every syllable carried not only the weight of the nation's aspirations but also the echoes of its rich history and the resolute spirit of its people.

In this cocoon of creativity, Hafeez Jalandhari emerged triumphant, presenting a lyrical masterpiece destined to resonate through the hearts of generations of Pakistanis. His thoughtful and deliberate approach ensured that every word of the anthem resonated not just in sound but in the profound essence of the nation it represented.

On that auspicious day in 1954, as the national anthem graced the airwaves of Radio Pakistan, sung by the very hand that meticulously penned its verses, it carried not just the soul but the revered craftsmanship of a nation sculpted by the poetic prowess of Hafeez Jalandhari during those three solitary months. His dedication elevated him beyond a poet, casting him as a master of poetry weaving the aspirations and identity of a nation into the fabric of time.

In a comprehensive portrayal of the poet Abul Asar Hafeez Jalandhari, the event in his honour, curated by Professor Ghaffar Shah, sheds light on the poet's notable achievements and contributions. Jalandhari showcased his poetic talent early on, composing his first poem, 'Mohammed ki Kashti,' at the age of seven. Commencing his literary journey in 1921 with 'Ejaz Jalandhar' and later co-editing 'Shahab' in 1922.

Jalandhari's contributions extended beyond poetry to patriotism, evident in his creation of morale-boosting songs for the army in Kashmir. His efforts during World War II garnered recognition from British India, resulting in the honorary title of "Khan Bahadur" bestowed upon him. However, in adherence to the poet's principles and in respect for Quaid-e-Azam's vision, he chose to relinquish this honor.

Among Jalandhari's notable works is his renowned 'Shahnama' (1926). This magnum opus is acclaimed for its widespread popularity, alongside his composition of the national anthem of Azad Kashmir. Jalandhari's versatility shines through in his ability to craft verses of both Nazm and Geet, which are easily adaptable to musical expression.

The event, expertly narrated by Professor Ghaffar Shah, under-scores Jalandhari's lasting legacy, emphasizing the resonance of his poetry with the public and its enduring adaptability to musical interpretation. Through 'Shahnama' and the national anthem, he solidified his place as a notable figure in Urdu literature and cultural heritage.

Golden Jubilee, Hafeez seen with family members:
daughters Fahmida (left) and Shamim (right)

VII

Family and Relationships

7

Family Relationships

Beyond the poet's creative pursuits, his personal life unfolded with fascinating twists. Even as a child, his family life was complex. As he grew up, he initially desired minimal responsibilities, but Jalandhari ended up in a difficult family situation, nonetheless. At a young age in his late teens, he understood the responsibility of supporting not only his mother and wife but also other relatives and their children, as well, through much struggle and strife.

The poet underwent multiple losses of family members, including his first daughter in Jalandhar. Hafeez became the father of seven daughters: Batool, Tasneem, Fahmida, Saeeda, Tahira, Shameem and Zia. He devoted poems to each of his daughters, which were included in various literature publications for children.

However, at times his fiery temper sparked conflicts. Jalandhari often found himself navigating the complexities of familial relationships. He married Anela, whom he had met during his stay in England and was initially his English Tutor. The decision to buy a house for Anela, his second wife and their daughter Zia, near the first wife's residence highlighted the unconventional dynamics in his family, symbolizing the evolution from a carefree existence to a life filled with tangled connections. Luckily, the daughters bonded closely to their youngest sibling, Zia.

These facets of the poet's personal life, from an early reluctance to shoulder responsibilities to managing a complex family with seven daughters, offer a deeper understanding of the man behind the poetry. It unveils a poet who not only shaped national anthems but also had to grapple with the complexities of human relationships and the evolving responsibilities that came with them.

His home nestled in the heart of Model Town Lahore, within the embrace of unique and traditional architecture, was an extraordinary residence meticulously crafted under his discerning gaze. Every carving, every pillar, and every detail was overseen with a poet's heart, as he envisioned a haven for his beloved wife, Zainab, and his cherished daughters.

This majestic home with pillars adorned with intricate details still stands as silent witnesses to the past and the poet's deep love and appreciation for the cultural heritage that permeates every corner. His name beautifully written above the address at the main gate opens the door to a unique story in time. It is a testament to Hafeez Jalandhari`s poetic sensibilities, where upon entering the gate stands a majestic fountain that whispers the soothing verses of his love for his family.

The courtyard, a vibrant canvas of colors with flowers, shrubs, and plants chosen with care, reflects not only the poet's connection to nature but also his desire to create a tranquil space for his loved ones. This enchanting oasis is not just a home; it is a love letter written in architecture.

Venturing further, the large veranda beckons, a testament to the poet's vision for moments spent with family under the comforting shade of carefully chosen trees. Here, Hafeez's gaze seems to have swept over the sprawling property, ensuring every inch would resonate with the warmth and poetry of familial bonds.

Amidst the carefully manicured landscape, fruit trees of every kind stand tall, bearing witness to the poet's desire to provide not just shelter, but a bounty of nature's gifts for his beloved family. The orchard, with its variety of fruit-laden branches, became a living metaphor for the poet's aspirations of abundance and prosperity for those he held dear.

As the sun sets and casts a golden hue over this poetic abode, one cannot help but feel the essence of Hafeez's love and dedication infused into every stone, every petal, and every fruit-bearing branch. This home is a testament to a poet's dream, where every detail is a verse in the symphony of love, and every corner echoes the timeless poetry of familial bonds.

His wife, Zainab, lived a life filled with responsibilities and surprises. The household thrived under her meticulous care, witnessing the changing seasons and the laughter of daughters blending harmoniously with nature's bounty in the courtyard.

Tahira, his daughter, recalls her father's protective embrace, extending beyond the walls of their home. Under his encouragement, she and her sisters ventured into new experiences, during family vacations in Kashmir. Their shared moments in places like Srinagar and Gulmarg were filled with joy and exploration, guided by the love and vision of their parents.

In the midst of verses penned by the poet, Zainab's silent narrative echoed—a tale of a woman who, with grace and resilience, cultivated a home where familial love bloomed amidst the beauty of nature. The household, alive with laughter and struggles, became a testament to Zainab's unwavering commitment and the enduring legacy of Hafeez Jalandhari's creativity.

PHOTOS OF FAMILY MEMBERS

Wife Zainab and daughter Shameem seen standing infront of the
Ancestral home 43-44 G Model Town

Daughter Tahira, mother of author Naveen, Mudassir and Yashar Khan

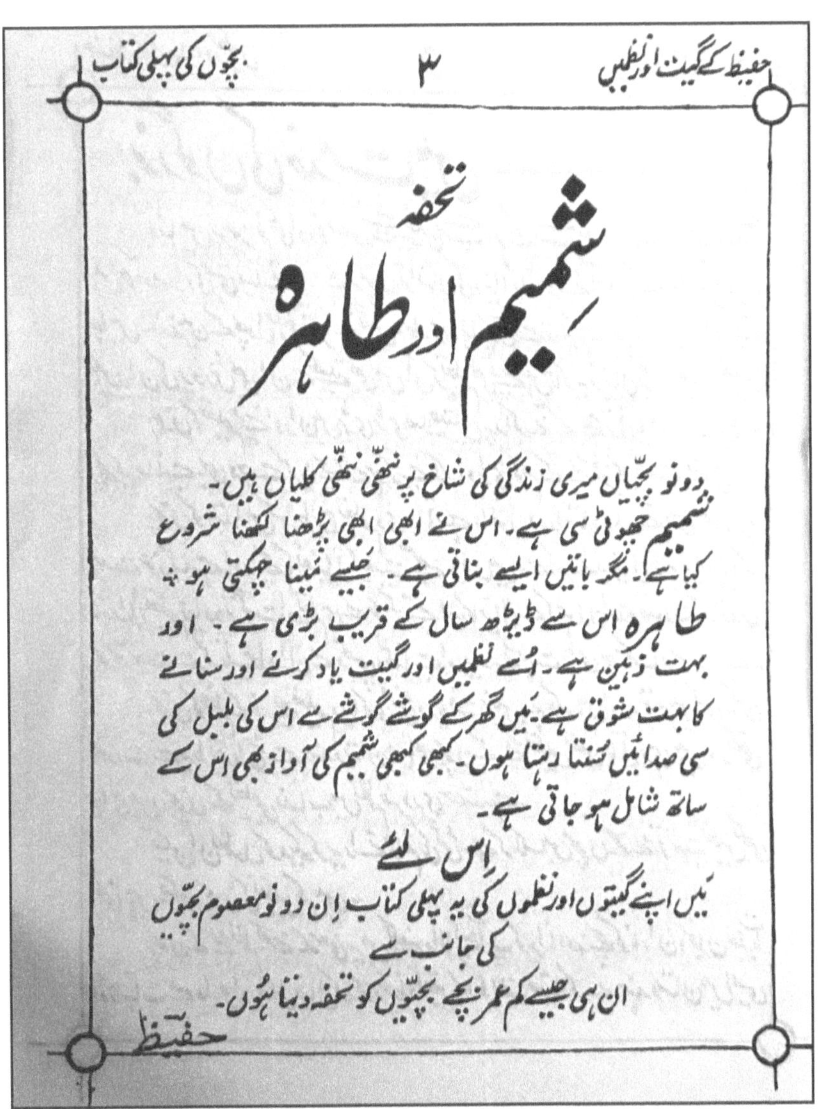

تحفہ

شمیم اور طاہرہ

دونو بچیاں میری زندگی کی شاخ پر ننھی ننھی کلیاں ہیں۔ شمیم چھوٹی سی ہے۔ اس نے ابھی ابھی پڑھنا لکھنا شروع کیا ہے۔ مگر باتیں ایسے بناتی ہے۔ جیسے نینا چھکتی ہو۔ طاہرہ اس سے ڈیڑھ سال کے قریب بڑی ہے۔ اور بہت ذہین ہے۔ اُسے نظمیں اور گیت یاد کرنے اور سنانے کا بہت شوق ہے۔ میں گھر کے گوشے گوشے سے اس کی بلبل کی سی صدائیں سنتا رہتا ہوں۔ کبھی کبھی شمیم کی آواز بھی اس کے ساتھ شامل ہو جاتی ہے۔

اس لئے

میں اپنے گیتوں اور نظموں کی یہ پہلی کتاب اِن دو نو معصوم بچوں کی جانب سے ان ہی جیسے کم عمر نچے بچوں کو تحفہ دیتا ہوں۔

حفیظ

A Poem written by Hafeez Jalandhari for his daughters Tahira and Shameem

Daughter Tasneem, mother of Mubaschir and Mohbeen Inayet.

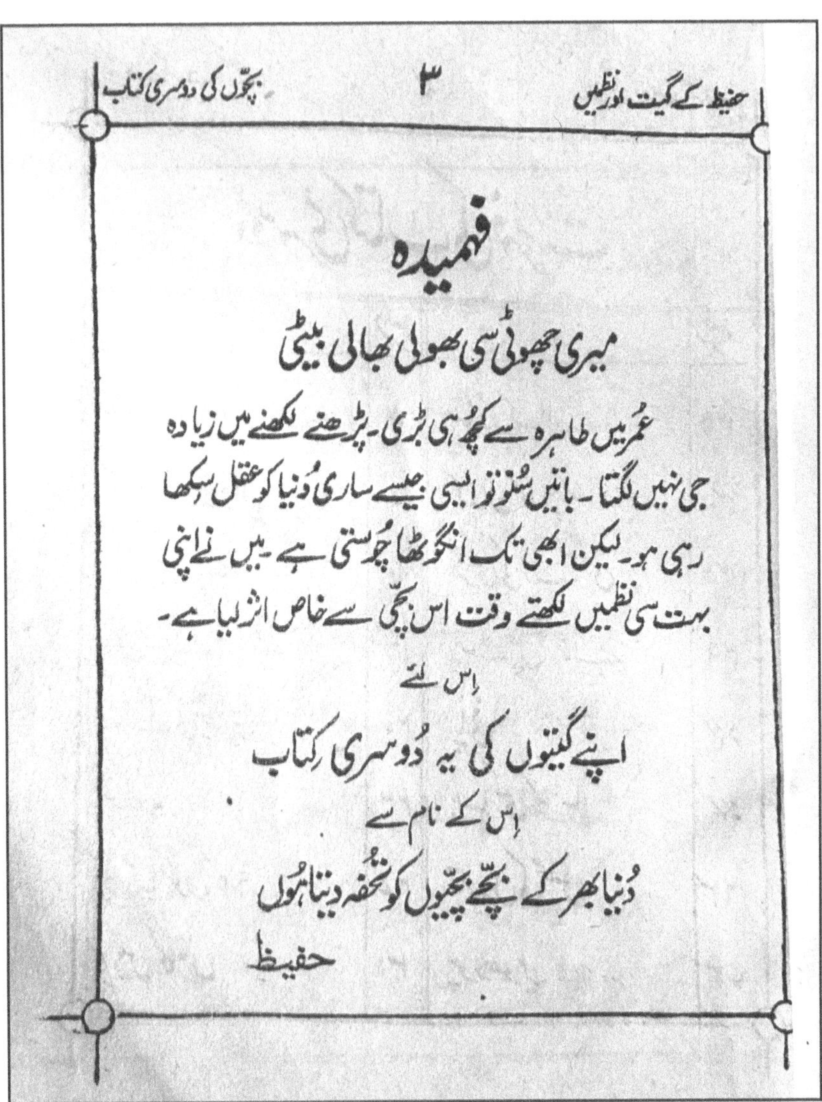

A poem written for by Hafeez for his daughter Fahmida

Daughter Saeeda Kausar

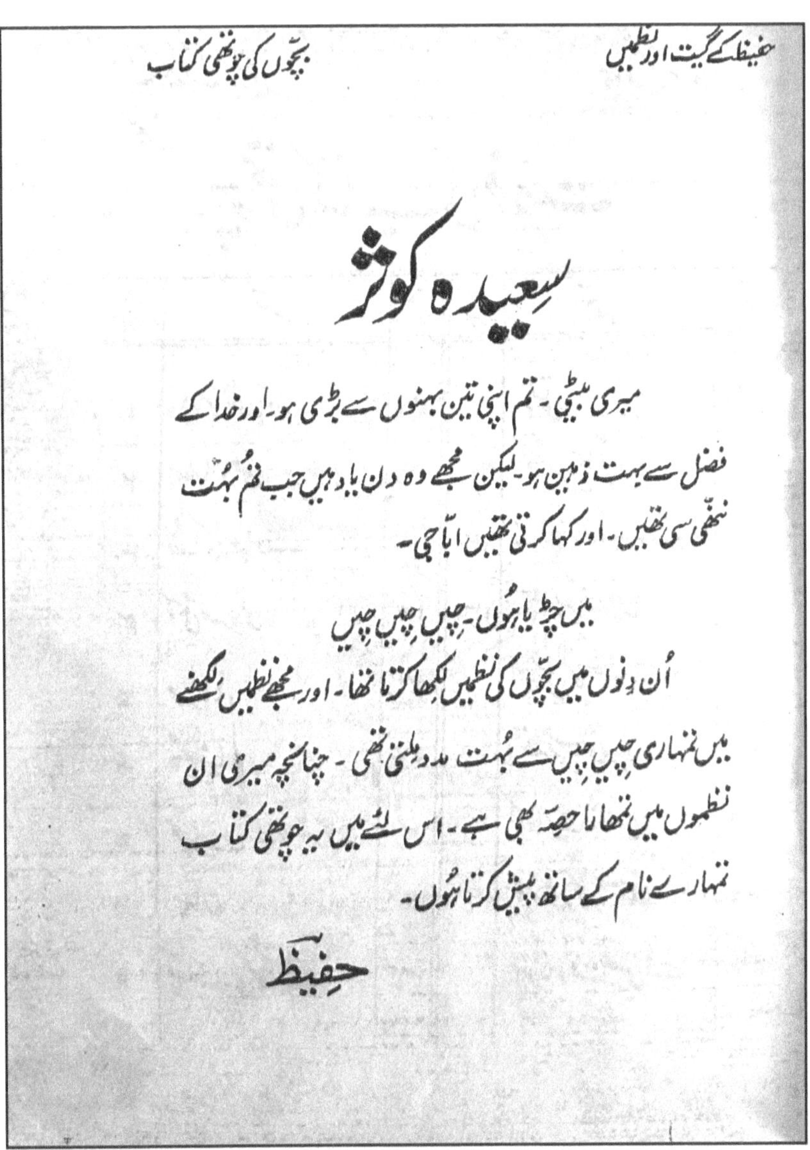

A Poem written by Hafeez Jalandhari for his daughter Saeeda Kausar.

Hafeez Jalandhari with his daughters-Fahmida (left)
mother of Basharat, Nabila, Kamran and Javedan Arshad
Daughter Shameem (right) mother of Meeral Mughal and Asad Abdullah
Daughter Zia (far right) mother of Sohail Hashmi and Wakar Siraj

Asad Abdullah and family standing in front of their ancestral home

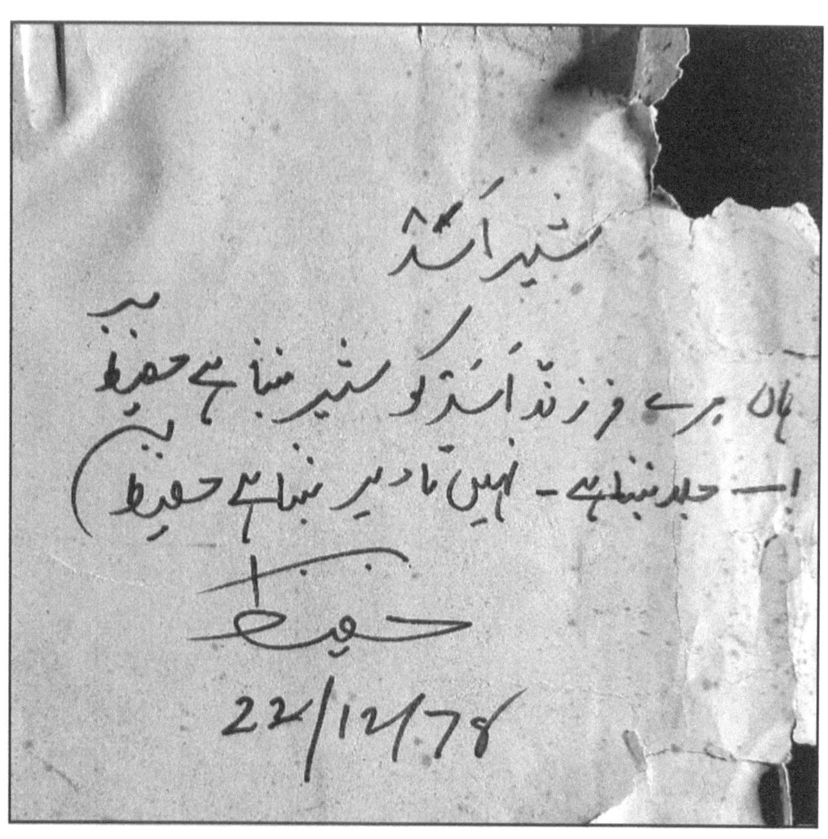

Poem written by Hafeez Jalandhari to his grandson Asad Abdullah

Abul Asar Hafeez Jalandhari, "Abbajaan"

Words cannot express a granddaughter's pride,
Of Good News brought to Grandfather's side,

He dreams I was born as a gift to Mother,
His wisdom and warmth matched by no other,

Bestowed by God that his voice should be heard,
Moving hearts and minds by ink and by word,

As God trials his servants testing their faith,
He arose to the challenge with fortitude and grace,
He forges in fire and through firm tribulation,
An anthem to energize the birth of a nation,

In musing with nature some solace he finds,
His expression portrays the greatest of minds,

An aura of eternity reflecting his craft,
"God is my friend", he smiled, and he laughed,

A legacy fashioned by word and by deed,
A love that lives on by blood and by seed,

Achiever of accolades and highest of prize,
"Yet more I must write", as he closes his eyes.

Basharat Arshad (Granddaughter) &
Omar Naseeb (Great-Grandson).

Abul Asar Hafeez Jalandhari, my grandfather, from his third daughter, Fahmida, was very loving and caring. But what fills me with awe and pride is the fact that a person who fell out of school from class four was so brilliant that he achieved eminence in the field of poetry and literature. I cannot recall any such personality who was self-educated and rose to this glory.

Kamran Arshad (Grandson).

Our Profound Poet of Pakistan

It is an honour to be mentioned in this reflective compilation of my great-grandfather's work.
There is no prouder moment than to witness the nation of Pakistan's children, similar to my own son's age, in every school, in every city standing upright to sing his Pak Sar Zameen.
As his powerful words rightly imply, 'Abhi to Mein Jawaan Hoon,' Hafeez Jalandhari does, indeed, live on, within all of us.
His legacy is passed down through the generations and his message continues.

Ayesha (Great-granddaughter).

In the words of his descendant,

"It is great that he is my great-great grandad"

~ Aadam

VIII

Literary Legacy

8

Published Works

Early Years and Literary Beginnings: Jalandhari embarked on his literary journey in 1922, serving as the editor for prestigious monthly magazines such as Nonehal, Hazar Dastaan, Teehzeeb-e-Niswan, and Makhzan, until 1929.

His poetic prowess came to light with the publication of his inaugural collection, "Nagma-e-Zar," in 1935, marking the onset of a remarkable literary career.

Contributions to the Pakistan Movement: Inspired by a fervent patriotism, Jalandhari actively participated in the Pakistan Movement, utilizing his writings as a powerful tool to rally support for the cause.

In 1946, his quest for cultural enrichment led him to the Sylhet region of Bengal, where he witnessed a captivating mushaira performance.

National Anthem and Musical Legacy: A defining moment occurred on 23 February, 1949 when Jalandhari's poetic genius shone brightly - his lyrics were selected to compose Pakistan's national anthem. He also penned the Kashmiri National Anthem (Azad Kashmir).

His unique contributions to Urdu poetry extended beyond the written word, as he was celebrated for the enchanting melody of his voice and the rhythmic beauty of his songs. Notably, 'Abhi Toh Mein Jawan Hoon' remains a timeless piece, echoing through the decades.

Diverse Artistic Expression: Beyond his patriotic verses, Jalandhari demonstrated a rich diversity in his poetic expressions. Despite being a devout Muslim, he wrote 'Krishn Kanhaiya,' a poem in praise of the Hindu god Krishna, showcasing his respect for the cultural mosaic of South Asia.

Professional and Political Engagements: Post-World War II, Jalandhari seamlessly transitioned into a role as the **Director of the Song Publicity Department**, leaving a lasting imprint on the musical landscape.

His commitment to the nation extended to active involvement in the armed forces, where he served as the **Director General of Morals.** Subsequently, he assumed a prominent **advisory role to President** Field Marshal Mohammad Ayub Khan and held a key position as **Director of the Writers Guild of Pakistan.**

Literary Masterpiece: Jalandhari's magnum opus, "Shahnam-e-Islam," stands as a testament to his literary prowess. Modeled after Firdowsi's Shahnameh, this work is a poetic chronicle of the glorious history of Islam, garnering him immense fame.

Personal Life: In 1917, at the age of 17, Jalandhari entered into matrimony with his cousin, Zainab Begum, and together they nurtured a family of six daughters. Later, in 1939, he ventured into a second marriage with Anela, a young English woman of Lithuanian descent; they had a daughter.

Legacy, Honors, and Departure: Jalandhari's contributions were duly recognized with prestigious awards, such as the Hilal-i-Imtiaz, and the Pride of Performance Award.

In 2001, the Pakistan Post Office paid homage to his enduring legacy by issuing a commemorative postage stamp in the 'Poets of Pakistan' series.

The final chapter his life unfolded in Lahore, Pakistan, on 21 December 1982, where he bid farewell at the age of 82. His final resting place, near the Minar-e-Pakistan, serves as a symbolic tribute to the essence of the Pakistan Resolution.

Quami Tarana
Pakistani National
Anthem

Shahnama-e-Islam
Hafeez Jalandhari
1929
Masnavi

Shahnaama-e-Islam
Hafeez Jalandhari
1937

Shahnama-e-Islam
Hafeez Jalandhari
1946
Masnavi

Shahnama-e-Islam
Hafeez Jalandhari
1960
Islamic History

Naghma-e-Zar
Hafeez Jalandhari
1932

Tasveer-e-Kashmir
Hafeez Jalandhari
1937
Nazm

Phool Mala
Hafeez Jalandhari
1928

Soz-o-Saaz
Hafeez Jalandhari
1945

Soz-o-Saz
Hafeez Jalandhari
1960

Bahar Ke Phool
Hafeez Jalandhari
1940
Nazm

Hafeez Jalandhari Ka Salam

Haft Paikar
Hafeez Jalandhari
1959
Short-story

In 2001, the Pakistan Post Office honored his enduring legacy with a commemorative postage stamp as part of the 'Poets of Pakistan' series, paying homage to his profound influence.

IX

Selected Verses and Poems by Hafeez Jalandhari

9

Selected Verses and Poems with short commentaries.

Hafeez Jallandhar wrote his lyrics in Urdu – the official language of Pakistan – but used words that are shared in the Persian (Farsi) language too, so that speakers of both languages could understand the national anthem of Pakistan.

In 1954, the resonant notes the Quami Tarana -'Pāk Sarzamīn,' meaning 'Thy Sacred Land,' echoed through the airwaves as Pakistan officially embraced it as its national anthem. This symbolic musical embodiment of patriotism took center stage after the nation's hard-fought independence in 1947.

Pakistani National Anthem- Qaumi Tarana

Paak sar zameen shaad baad
Kishwari haseen shaad baad
Too nishaani azmi aalee shaan Arzi Pakistan!
Markazi yaqeen shaad baad

Paak sar zameen kaa nizaam
Quwwati ukhuwwati awaam
Qaum, Mulk, Saltanat Paayindah taabindah baad!
Shaad baad manzili muraad

Parcami sitaarah o hilaal
Rahbari taraqqee o kamaal
Tarjumaani maazee shaani haal Jaani istaqbaal!
Saayahyi Khudaayi zu al-jalaal

An English translation of the anthem:

Blessed be the sacred land, Happy be the bounteous realm,
Symbol of high resolve, Land of Pakistan.
Blessed be thou citadel of faith.
The Order of this Sacred Land

Is the might of the brotherhood of the people.
May the nation, the country, and the State
Shine in glory everlasting.
Blessed be the goal of our ambition.

This flag of the Crescent and Star
Leads the way to progress and perfection.
Interpreter of our past, glory of our present, Inspiration of our future.
Symbol of Almighty's protection.

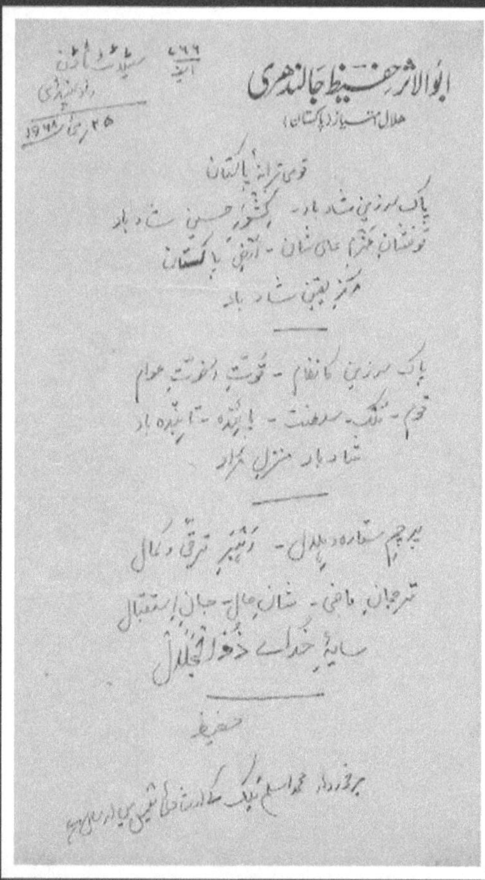

The original handwritten version of the national anthem of Pakistan by Abul Asar Hafeez Jalandhari

Nestled in South Asia, sharing borders with India, Afghanistan, Iran, and China, Pakistan, despite its youth, boasts a history and culture spanning over eight and a half millennia. From its roots in the British Indian Empire in 1858, the journey to sovereignty unfolded in 1947, driven by the Pakistan Movement advocating for a distinct home for Muslims within British India. The official constitution emerged in 1956, and in 1971, the birth of Bangladesh marked the transformation of East Pakistan.

As the echoes of independence reverberated, Pakistan sought an anthem to harmonize its spirit. An enticing reward of 5,000 rupees was announced for the lyricist and composer who could capture the essence of the nation. Despite initial attempts, the search proved futile, leading to the establishment of the National Anthem Committee (NAC) in December 1948.

The NAC, on a mission to craft an original anthem, faced delays. By January 1950, during the Indonesian President's visit, Pakistan still lacked its anthem. Urgency struck as the government pushed the NAC to unveil a composition for the impending visit of the Shah of Iran later that year.

Amidst the search, composer Ahmed G. Chagla's melody surfaced, earning approval on 21 August 1950 as Pakistan's official music for the anthem. Initially, the anthem only featured an instrumental rendition, awaiting fitting lyrics. The NAC reached out to renowned Pakistani poets, receiving an abundance of submissions. Hafeez Jalandhari's words emerged victorious out of 733 submissions, and on 13 August 1954, the national anthem debuted on Radio Pakistan, with Hafeez voicing the lyrics himself, marking a harmonious celebration of Pakistan's identity.

Author of Pakistani national anthem, Hafeez Jalandhari directing the live recording of the anthem on Radio Pakistan

Abhi To Main Jawan Hun (I Am Still Young)

In this poem Hafeez champions the importance of embracing the present moment. Musical imagery is woven throughout, describing a melody that ignites emotions. The repeated assertion, "I am still young," reflects a defiance against the passage of time and a plea to live in the present. Ultimately, the poem weaves together nature, rebellion, love, and the fleeting nature of life, encouraging an appreciation for the richness of experiences.

 ABUL ASAR HAFEEZ JALANDHARI

Abhi To Main Jawan Hun (I Am Still Young)

The air is delightful, the flowers are in bloom,
There's a melody in the air, Spring is in full swing.
Where has the cupbearer gone? Come back, come back this way.
Look, who is watching? The dawn is breaking slowly.
Rise, rise, O cupbearer! Fill the cup, fill it and bring it here,
Turn your gaze towards the garden, look at the ambiance, be aware.
Look at those dark clouds, they have gathered on the horizon.

It's a gathering of wine drinkers, the wine house is in full swing.
What arrogance is this, so disdainful? Understand me, O ignorant one.
The idea of asceticism, where is it now? I am still young.
The mention of worship is there, concern for salvation too,
Passion has its rewards; the thought is a torment.

But listen, O wise one, you too have peculiar things,
Youth and love have been different sometimes.
Beautiful and alluring, expressions full of mischief,
The air is fragrant, why not be passionate?

Artists of mischief, some here, some there,
They rise to revelry, what can anyone do
Come, let's hear a brief tale, your point of view,
If it's correct, then fine, But I am still young.

This wandering, searching, this exploration of heights,
The chirping of nightingales, the laughter of the flower-faced ones.
If there is a connection with someone, worries and thoughts are lost,
Sometimes when destiny sleeps, the one who laughs starts crying.

These are the stories of love, these are the youth-filled moments,
From there, there is kindness, from here, there is harshness.
This sky, this earth, the heart-captivating sights,
They make life enchanting, should I leave them here?
Death is so harsh, I won't believe it, No, no, not yet I am still young.

No grief of release or restraint, neither of high nor low,
Not of the bad or good, nor of the promise of the past.
Hope and despair lost, feelings lost, reason lost,
Surrounded by obscurity, except for the glass, everything is lost.
May there be no lack in the wine, may there be companionship in
the cup,
May this gathering continue, may we remain in harmony.

That melody played by the musician,
The atmosphere of music, the pain of the heart,
The impact of the musical sound, ignite a fire in the liver,
On every lip, there should be a cry, don't stop, O cupbearer,
Keep pouring, keep pouring, I am still young.

Commentary: To delve deeper into this poetic text, there is a celebration of the vibrant beauty of spring, portraying blooming flowers and a melodic atmosphere. The poet expresses a longing for the return of the cupbearer, symbolizing a desire for the pleasures of life. There is a rejection of asceticism and a bold embrace of youth, challenging societal norms.

The verses highlight the allure of love and passion, describing them as beautiful and alluring, filled with mischief. The text explores contrasts, including joy and sorrow, laughter and tears, creating a nuanced portrayal of the human experience. The poet shares a desire for the continuation of gatherings, emphasizing the importance of wine, companionship, and harmony.

Musical imagery is woven throughout, describing a melody that ignites emotions. The repeated assertion, "I am still young," reflects a defiance against the passage of time and a plea to live in the present. Ultimately, the poem weaves together nature, rebellion, love, and the fleeting nature of life, encouraging an appreciation for the richness of experiences and the importance of embracing the moment.

Bondage

The poem, titled "Bondage," offers a poignant reflection on the devastating impact of slavery on the human spirit. Overall, "Bondage" is a compelling exploration of the multifaceted and insidious consequences of slavery on the individual and society.

BONDAGE

Slavery kills the sentiment of honour
It deadens the courage to bear hardship.
Self-respect loses its meaning for a slave.
With the collar of contempt round his neck he feels happy.

Slavery frightens man away from the heights of aspirations.
It teaches him the art of crawling on his belly.
Slaves see danger in everything see.
Fear governs them in peace, and flight guides them in war.

Slaves have not the stamp of firmness on their will
Their hearts are not drawn to the charms of steadfastness.
Slavery robs man of his humanity.
Action is there but without the beauty of conviction.

Slavery murders true values and is the enemy of thought.
It is opposed to self-realization and is hostile to God's worship.
Slavery is devoid of wisdom and is incapable of true love.
It courts ease and seeks satisfaction in lust.

In the battle of life trembling at the enemy's sword
Slaves cut their throats with their own hands.
Their eyes see not beyond the realm of doubt.
And are curtained from Reality.
Slavery with its own hands forges its charms.
And thus, bedecked makes merry.

 Abul Asar Hafeez Jalandhari

Commentary: In his poem the poet vividly describes the erosion of essential qualities such as honor, courage, and self-respect in the face of enslavement. The imagery of a collar of contempt symbolizes the dehumanizing effect of bondage, portraying a paradox where the oppressed may find a perverse sense of contentment.

The poet emphasizes the debilitating consequences of slavery on aspirations and character, portraying slaves as individuals who have been conditioned to fear boldness and shy away from genuine self-expression. The absence of firmness in their will and the lack of steadfastness in their hearts underscore the profound devaluation of humanity caused by slavery.

The poem also delves into the spiritual and intellectual consequences of enslavement, asserting that slavery is not only an affront to human dignity but also a hindrance to genuine thought, self-realization, and worship. The verses suggest that slavery distorts values, promotes superficial pleasures, and obstructs the pursuit of wisdom and true love.

The concluding lines employ powerful metaphors, highlighting the tragic fate of those enslaved, who, in the battle of life, inadvertently contribute to their own demise. The metaphorical blindness to reality and the forging of charms by slavery's own hands serve as powerful images of the self-destructive nature of oppression.

AUTUMN LAMENT

The poem "Autumn Lament" is a poignant and introspective poem that uses the metaphor of an autumn leaf in the garden of life to convey a sense of melancholy and loss.

AUTUMN LAMENT

I am an autumn leaf in the garden of Life.
Cherished by Whirlwinds and loved by Sandstorms.
In one night only the smiles of joy came to this end.
In the morning every bud in bloom had become a tearful eye
What had become of the treasures of One who gives Sustenance to
both the Worlds!

I am given only grief, that too by someone else.
I am not longing for eternal life.
I pray only for unexpected death.
Each bud, out of fright, appeared to me like a cage.
Each leaf deluded me as though it were the hand of a hunter.
Where there is no feeling of captivity,
It is impossible to expect release.
Such prisoners do not even want to know
For how long they are imprisoned.

ABUL ASAR HAFEEZ JALANDHARI

Commentary: "Autumn Lament" reflects on the transient nature of joy and the inevitable passage of time, drawing on imagery in nature to depict the fragility of existence.

The initial lines set the tone, by portraying the poet as an autumn leaf, suggesting a stage in life characterized by maturity and perhaps decline. The metaphorical use of whirlwinds and sandstorms as entities that cherish and love the leaf adds a touch of complexity, hinting at the paradoxical nature of life's challenges and adversities.

The abrupt shift from smiles of joy to tearful eyes overnight conveys a sudden and unexpected change in fortune. A juxtaposition of blooming buds turning into tearful eyes evokes a sense of loss and the ephemeral nature of happiness.

The poem then takes a philosophical turn by questioning the fate of the treasures provided by the giver of sustenance to both worlds. This may allude to a broader existential contemplation about the purpose and meaning of life, especially in the face of adversity.

The poet expresses a profound sense of grief, emphasizing that it is imposed by someone else, introducing an element of external agency in the experience of suffering. The desire for unexpected death, rather than eternal life, reflects a longing for release from the burdens and sorrows of existence.

The imagery of buds appearing like cages and leaves resembling the hands of a hunter adds layers of metaphorical depth to the speaker's perception of the world. These metaphors suggest a sense of entrapment and deception, highlighting the speaker's feeling of vulnerability and disillusionment.

The concluding lines, about prisoners who do not want to know the duration of their imprisonment, further underscore the theme of resignation and acceptance in the face of life's uncertainties. "Autumn Lament" is a reflection on the complexities of human emotions and the inevitable journey through life's seasons, resonating with themes of impermanence, existential questioning, and the acceptance of fate.

KRISHNA THE BELOVED

Behold the Beauty is a poem that delves into the symbolic and profound aspects of Lord Krishna, a revered deity in Hinduism. The opening lines introduce Krishna as an embodiment of imagination and lofty thought, transcending the physical realm and residing in the divine and spiritual sphere. The poem explores the symbolic nature of Krishna's form, hinting at the essence of nature and portraying a divine and supernatural existence.

KRISHNA THE BELOVED

Oh, beholders, behold this beauty,
Understand this secret, this imprint of imagination,
This lofty thought, this embodiment of radiance,
This image of Krishna.

It implies a form, it hints at nature,
It is apparent, yet concealed,
Near or far, is it fire or light?
Distinct from the world, he with the flute,
The cowherd of Gokul.

It is the magic of miracles, revealing secrets slowly,
What a grandeur, oh God, what a pride, oh God.
I am amazed, what a unique glory, a dancing Krishna in the court,
Within the idol-house, the idol of beauty,
Transformed into reality, those elevated sights,

All memories flooding back, by the banks of the Jamuna.
The swaying of greenery, the fragrance of flowers,
Dark, looming clouds, intoxicated breezes,
Innocent desires, waves of love,
With the milkmaids, hands entwined,
A dance in Brijnath's honor.

In the flute's melody, there's intoxication, not wine,
It's something else entirely, a spirit dancing,
An ecstasy trembling, a mind engrossed in wine,
Consciousness intoxicated.

A sword of lightning, a joyful cry,
A weeping joy, proud love,
Enchanted beauty, a magical spell,
In the court alone, helpless is Krishna,
Come, O dark one, all lovers are in awe,
This is the beloved's rule.

All have become cowardly, the veil doesn't exist,
For the sake of honor, come, my dark one,
In the brilliance of India, hide in my embrace,
There's strife now, and the battlefield is heated,
Ghalib is Duryodhan, Jagdish has arrived,
Worries have disappeared, Arjuna is called,
A message is delivered, what's the sorrow of the sorrowful,
What's the sorrow of the master?

Behold the plan, fate has been made,
The sword has been drawn, the conduct is hostile,
The appearance is dazzling, the heart is sentiment-invoking,
When anger arrives, lightning strikes,
And joy descends, even homes are looted.

Among fairies is Gulfam, for Radha, there is Shyam,
Balram's brother, residing in Mathura,
Kanhaiya in Vrindavan, the brave has become ruins,
The garden is destroyed, the companions are troubled,
By the banks of the Jamuna, it's all silent,

The storm is silent, no enthusiasm in the waves,
Only the flame has touched you, this desire is all that remains.

O king of India, come once again,
Erase sorrow and pain, with clouds and breeze,
With the nightingale's call, with the splendor of flowers,
With the magic of enchantment, with the tumult of sorrow,
With the tumult of battle, with the pain of separation,
Mathura is not pleased, if you come, glory comes,
If you come, life comes, do not come alone,
Let the festivities be together, with the mischief of friends.

Oh, beholders, behold this beauty,
Understand this secret, this imprint of imagination,
This lofty thought, this embodiment of radiance,
This image of Krishna.

Commentary: Poet Hafeez Jalandhar penned both Pakistani and Kashmiri national anthems, as well as an Islamic magnus opus: he surprised many when his extraordinary poem on the Hindu Deity, Krishna was discovered. In pre-partion times, Indian festivals, like Janmasthami and Dussehra, were also celebrated by people of Muslim faith.

Couplets and poems in Urdu on Hindu deities were not that uncommon at all. Central to the imagery is Krishna as the flute-playing cowherd of Gokul, symbolizing the pastoral and carefree aspects of divinity. The flute's melody becomes a metaphor for spiritual intoxication, emphasizing a connection that goes beyond mundane pleasures. The verses evoke the divine dance of Krishna in Brijnath's honor, portraying a celebration of love and innocence between the divine and devotees.

The poem employs metaphors, like the sword of lightning, joyful cries, and weeping joy, to capture the paradoxical nature of Krishna's presence. These symbols represent the simultaneous fierceness and tenderness of divine love, expressing the multifaceted emotions experienced in the presence of the beloved deity.

Symbolic characters, like Ghalib as Duryodhan and Jagdish are introduced, possibly representing internal conflicts or struggles within the poet's consciousness. The references to the destruction of the garden and a silent storm by the banks of the Jamuna symbolize the upheavals and challenges faced on the spiritual path, suggesting a contemplative state of the soul.

The poem concludes with a passionate call for Krishna's return, associating it with the alleviation of sorrow and pain. This call symbolizes the devotee's yearning for divine intervention, emphasizing the significance of Krishna's presence in bringing joy, life, and festivities. Overall, "Krishna, the Beloved" invites contemplation on the deep spiritual and emotional dimensions associated with the revered deity in Hinduism.

THE SOUL

The poem, "Soul", explores themes related to the soul, love, faith, and the transformative power of inner redemption. The poem also explores the transformative power of the soul, the redemptive nature of love, and the potential for personal awakening to have a positive impact on the world. The language is rich in metaphors and spiritual imagery, drawing on themes of faith, love, and the eternal nature of the soul.

THE SOUL

House thy unflickering lamp of love,
O way-lost dupe, relume the olden flame
In the wistful temple of dreams nurse in faith's grove
The memorial rose of peace no thorn can shame.

Delivered from thy passions' lurid gleams
And shadowing greed, for in the guise of friends,
Know: in the deep of hush the soul redeems:
She is the vanguard morn to darkness sends.

Her children in gloom, thy Motherland mourns and sighs,
Play Beauty's flute, like Krishna: thou art He.
If thou wilt wake, the world, aquiver, shall rise
And mitred priests of love will sing with thee.

Hate never pays, though sorrows purify,
Be posed in thy Self of love: incarnate, free.
If she resigns, who shall reveal the sky?
Soul's night is defeat: her dawn-sure victory.

Commentary: Opening Stanzas: "House thy unflickering lamp of love": The poet seems to suggest that the essence of one's being, or soul is like an enduring lamp of love that should be preserved or nurtured.

"O way-lost dupe, relume the olden flame": The poet addresses someone who may have lost their way and encourages them to reignite the flame of a past love or passion.

"In the wistful temple of dreams nurse in faith's grove / The memorial rose of peace no thorn can shame": These lines evoke a sense of longing and encourage the nurturing of faith and inner peace, symbolized by a thornless rose.

Liberation from Negative Influences: "Delivered from thy passions' lurid gleams / And shadowing greed, for in the guise of friends": The poet speaks about liberation from negative influences, such as passions and greed, often disguised as friendly connections.

The Soul's Redemptive Power: "Know: in the deep of hush the soul redeems: / She is the vanguard morn to darkness sends": The poem emphasizes the redemptive power of the soul during moments of stillness and quiet. The soul is portrayed as the herald of dawn, bringing light to darkness.

Connection to Motherland and Beauty: "Her children in gloom, they Motherland mourns and sighs, / Play Beauty's flute, like Krishna: thou art He": There's a connection between the people and their homeland, where even in dark times, the invocation of beauty is compared to the divine music played by Krishna, suggesting a spiritual and uplifting aspect.

Awakening and Global Impact: "If thou wilt wake, the world, aquiver, shall rise / And mitred priests of love will sing with thee": The poem suggests that an individual's awakening has the potential to impact the world positively, causing a ripple effect of love and harmony.

The Futility of Hate and the Power of Love: "Hate never pays, though sorrows purify, / Be posed in thy Self of love: incarnate, free": The poet argues against the futility of hate, suggesting that love is the true essence of existence and encourages being grounded in a self of love.

The Significance of the Soul: "If she resigns, who shall reveal the sky? / Soul's night is defeat: her dawn-sure victory": The poet contemplates the importance of the soul, portraying its resignation as a defeat and emphasizing its inevitable victory in the dawn of a new day.

AFRANGI KI DUNYA – THE WORLD OF THE WEST

The poem "Afrangi Ki Dunya - The World of the West" reflects on the multifaceted nature of the Western world, painting it as a kaleidoscopic talisman.

AFRANGI KI DUNYA — THE WORLD OF THE WEST

It is a kaleidoscopic Talisman—The world of the "Afrangi"
Destiny has shown me a glimpse of its modernity,
A world of dance and merriment, of sweet tunes and melody,
of bustle and panic, of disturbance and war,
A paradise, yet not without fear, If not quite real, still not all imaginary.

I see the horizon thick with clouds of trouble,
Days and nights of anxiety, mornings and evenings full of concern,
I see the art of destruction of Nations—
It is painful to watch, but you must see it,
It is impossible to describe all there is to see,
My eyes cannot discharge the function of the tongue.

Not earth alone but fire, water, and air as well,
Appear to be subjugated by man, with chains on their feet.
There is an earthquake underground as well as in the sky.
Angels look upon it with amazement and God Himself is its Witness.
Breaches have been made in the walls of eternity,

And Sway over Death itself is within the grasp of man.
It is not for me a poet, to philosophize,
The weight of solid results presses heavily on my mind,
In the civilization of man, be it new or old,
What I look for is 'beauty' and the beauty of the essence of things.
I have no enmity with the children of God—
That is to say, in my world there is no 'foreigner'.

Now that the Sun is shedding its splendor on the West,
For some time, the East has to suffer in darkness,
The dawn will come there, when this night passes,
Only those revolutions of time, neither you nor I have control.
The changes of night and day and the month and the year will continue.
These turns will last as long as the Heavenly orbs resolve.

The East is not devoid of learning and excellence,
There was a time when the West begged at its door for light.
However, the West has developed one peculiarity,
With which the efforts of the East have not been able to compete—
That peculiarity is its pride in the beauty of women,
This feature holds my East in fascination.

The market owes it activity to her,
The shops are attractive as she is there,
Bargains and business are brisk through her power,
Pockets jingle with coins of gold, for her to hear.
Advertisements at the turning of every lane point to her.
And on every wall her portrait is visible.
The colour of the wine and the cup of wine-shops is borrowed from her.

The red wine is but a reflection of her blood,
On the canvas of the picture, you see her work,
In the pages of the newspapers, you find her name.
She is in accord with the harp of Statecraft,
This is a secret which is seldom revealed.

I was struck with wonder when I saw the seaside.
The grains of sand had become the stars of the sky of beauty.
Blazing lights—like the glare of a bare sword in the Sun.
The dance, the song, the fun and the frolic.
Like waves of quicksilver trembling in water,
Were the waves of the world-brightening Sun in the Sea.

The West is, in reality, under the rule of the beautiful.
The Black and White are under their yoke,
The destruction of others is for their benefit,
The armies and soldiers are for their sake.
If nations are faces with guns—O, Beauty
It is to provide comfort for thee.

Commentary: To further delve into the poem, the poet acknowledges glimpses of modernity, describing a world filled with dance, merriment, sweet tunes, and melody, but also with elements of disturbance, panic, and war. The West is portrayed as a paradise tinged with fear, a complex reality that is neither entirely real nor imaginary.

Symbolically, the thick clouds on the horizon represent troubles, anxiety, and concerns that loom over this world. The poet observes the destructive tendencies of nations, witnessing the pain of such destruction but finding it challenging to articulate the full extent of what is seen. The poem suggests a sense of helplessness in conveying the depth of the turmoil witnessed.

The reference to the subjugation of earth, fire, water, and air by man, with chains on their feet, symbolizes the mastery humanity has achieved over the elements through technological advancements. The breaches in the walls of eternity and the sway over death itself highlight the profound impact of human progress and the manipulation of natural forces.

The poem contrasts the beauty and essence of things sought by the poet with the weight of solid results and the civilization of man, emphasizing a preference for intrinsic beauty over material achievements. The poet expresses a lack of enmity toward the "children of God," indicating an inclusive worldview where there is no concept of foreigners.

The reference to the Sun shedding its splendor on the West and the subsequent darkness in the East suggests a temporal imbalance, emphasizing the cyclical nature of time and the inevitability of change. The poet predicts a dawn in the East when this night passes, acknowledging the uncontrollable revolutions of time.

A notable aspect is the admiration for the West's pride in the beauty of women, a feature that the poet finds fascinating and distinctive. This admiration is not devoid of a hint of criticism, pointing out the West's unique focus on this aspect as something that sets it apart from the East.

The closing lines celebrate the dominance of beauty in the West, portraying it as a force that influences everything from markets and businesses to statecraft. The poem concludes with a reflection on the seaside, using vivid imagery to describe the captivating and powerful influence of beauty in the Western world, suggesting that beauty holds a significant sway over societal structures, even to the point of shaping nations and their armed forces.

Hafeez seen in a group photo
to support philanthropy projects, Pakistan.

X

Acknowledgements and Reflections

10

Acknowledgements and Reflections

In closing, Hafeez's tribute serves as a poignant reminder of the profound impact of Sir Abdul Qadir's patronage and friendship had on both his life and work. It was with the deepest respect that Hafeez presented, a tribute to his greatest and sincerest patron and friend the Hon'ble Sir Abdul Qadir with the following words in an edition of his collective poems.

Tribute to Sir Abdul Qadir

The gardener's eyes happened to fall on a wild-growing plant. He was pleased to see it, and thought that if this plant was nurtured, it would certainly bear fruit. With this idea uppermost in his mind he began to tend to this wild-growing plant along with others he had planted himself and protected them from all kinds of earthly calamities.

The result of this paternal care on the part of the gardener was that this plant, which remained uncared for such a long time, began to blossom forth and to yield fruit. This plant had now become a strong tree, but its branches were bent owing to the burden of gratitude that lay heavy upon them. However, its fruits both ripe and unripe were there to be the source of delight and pleasure to the gardener.

Hafeez Jalandhari

Contributions by Anela Pokukaitis and daughter Zia Siraj Hafeez

I would like to express my deepest gratitude to Anela and my Aunt Zia for their dedicated efforts in preserving the materials used to write this biography. Their meticulous work has illuminated the life and works of the eminent poet Hafeez Jalandhari, allowing me to share his poetic brilliance with a global audience. The task of gathering information and translating materials posed numerous challenges, but Anela's commitment and passion for this project were unwavering. Special thanks to Sir Abdul Qadir, Mr. Riaz Qadir, Syed Nazeer Niyazi, and Pandit Hali Chand Akhtar for their valuable contributions as explained and shared by Anela.

Hafeez Son Poet of India as written by Anela Podukaitis

The fertile land of India has for centuries been producing the most distinguished personalities, who have held positions envied in all lands and spheres of life: art, poetry, philosophy, architecture, astronomy and fine art, all have cultivated their genius. In the field of Urdu literature Wali, Sauda, Mir Taqi, Anis and Ghalib all have held the torch in turn and enriched the Urdu language. Down to the present age, Hali and Iqbal have achieved fame for their dynamic thoughts of sweet poetic expression.

The Indian subcontinent has been a mingling pot of different cultures and civilizations, but in spite of it all even today one thing remains crystal clear that the Indian touch in serenity of language and the melodious way of expression is a factor common all of poets of note, irrespective of their caste, and creed.

In my exploration I am introducing Hafeez to a global world with many languages from East to West, North to South. For he has captured the hearts not only of the people originally from the Indian subcontinent, now India and Pakistan-young and old, but Hindus and Muslims alike. The medium in which he writes is the mother tongue of millions of men (Humanity).

The collection of facts and materials for this biography was no means an easy task. The difficulties of language, in superbly as they seemed to start with, were gotten over by the help of friends who admired Hafeez and his work.

I must thank Sir Abdul Qadir and Mr. Riaz Qadir for some very able translations and also Syed Nazeer Niyazi and Pandit Hali Chand Akhtar who enriched my collections of materials by relating anecdotes, for which I am grateful to them.

Reference to his titles:

Malik-U-Shuara

Hassan-ul-Mul Bahadur

Firdausi-i-Islam

Abul Asar Hafeez Jalandhari, titles 'King of Poets.'

ANELA

Photo of Anela and Sohail Hashmi
(son of daughter Zia)

Nana

Tribute by Sohail Hashmi

Abu Al-Asar Hafeez Jalandhari was my grandfather from my mother's side. I used to call him Nana Jan.

Anela, was my Nani, (grandmother from my mother's side) and was Hafeez Jalandhari's second wife, who was from European descent. I used to call her 'Bari Mummy' (Bari meaning big, in a respectful way)

I was born in 1962. By then, Hafeez and Anela were divorced and living separate lives in Pakistan. Hafeez was still living in Model Town Lahore Pakistan, and Anela was living in Guru Mandir, Karachi, Pakistan

I was born and raised in London, UK, as my parents had been settled there since the early 1960's and I was lucky enough to be able to visit Pakistan from time to time as my parents sent me there, and there was a time when I even lived in Karachi for a year with my Nani Anela in Karachi who I adore till this day. My Nani Anela made me feel completely loved. It is a beautiful feeling that I will take with me till I am no more. I think that most Nani's (grandmothers) are like that with their daughters' children.

I remember one my first meetings with my Nana Hafeez Jaland-hari as a young boy in 1968. I must have been 6 or 7 years old. He was lying in a hospital bed in Lahore recovering from some illness, and I had been told by my mother that the President of Pakistan, General Ayub Khan had just visited my Nana 15 minutes ago to enquire about his health.

As I met my Nana in his hospital bed smiling at me, I felt a really nice feeling from him, and to everybody's shock and surprise, I jumped on his bed and lay next to him. My mother quickly tried to approach me to get me off the hospital bed, as Nana was laughing out aloud and he stopped her from pulling me off the bed. He then smiled at me and put his hand on my head and told my mother that I was a very confident little boy. Everyone laughed, and there started a new friendship with my Nana Hafeez Jalandhari.

Two week later when Nana was back home in Model Town Lahore and he had recovered from his ailment, our friend-ship had matured over this short time, and he took me hand in hand across two streets to attend a local wedding. What he said to me that day, I will never forget. As we approached the wedding residence, I saw a lot of people standing outside the wedding house, and I asked my Nana "what are all these people were doing outside the wedding house?" You see, being a little British Pakistani boy, living in Streatham London SW16,

I had no idea that these were poor people who were waiting for excess food to be given to them after the wedding would be over. I remember my Nana speaking to me in Urdu, which I understood as my parents made me speak Urdu in our London home. He said looking at me straight in the eyes "We are who we are, but these are the real people of Pakistan; it is our duty to look after them, to feed them and to educate them, as they are our people, the people of Pakistan!" These words have stayed with me ever since that moment in 1968.

Moving forward to my teenage years in London, it must have been around 1974 and my Nana was travelling from Lahore to London to stay with us as he was booked for many Urdu 'Mushairas' (poetry recitals) in London and in Birmingham.

My Nana, now being older and being a little eccentric, having written many books and creating a lot of poetry had achieved more than most men at his age. He was also highly respected for writing the National Anthem for Pakistan and also for Azad Kashmir, as well as having written the Shahnama-e-Islam and other notable works.

One day, as I passed by his room, I heard a sound of sobbing. Intrigued and concerned, I entered to find him in tears. His vulnerability struck me. "They don't understand," he uttered. Curious, I probed further, only to discover a profound revelation. The Shahnama-e-Islam, one of his monumental works, was not entirely his creation. According to Nana, he merely held the pen; the instructions flowed from above, a divine intervention guiding his hand.

The revelation left me in awe, realizing the depth of his connection to his craft. As a young teenager, I grappled with the

ABUL ASAR HAFEEZ JALANDHARI

concept of divine inspiration shaping literary masterpieces. In that moment, I witnessed the vulnerability of a man who had created not just poetry, but a legacy that transcended the earthly realm.

Till this day, I carry with me the lessons imparted by my Nana Hafeez Jalandhari. Beyond the celebrated poet, he was a grandfather who intertwined the threads of tradition, duty, and divine connection. As I reflect on those moments of laughter, tears, and profound insights, I recognize the enduring impact of a man whose pen echoed the whispers of a higher realm, leaving behind a legacy that continues to inspire generations.

Written by
Sohail Hashmi

Abstract Artist/Television Producer|
Director|Actor|TV Anchor/Host|
Marketing Director|RadioPresenter|Publisher|
Writer |Content Creator|Broadcaster|
Brand Ambassador|Voice-over Artist |
Documentary Film Maker|Writer|
Master of Ceremony |SH & Associates |
Digital Media services

Tribute

By the Inayet family,

This book serves as a personal and intimate account of the exemplary life of Great Grandpa; whose conviction, truth and art led the way to a new form of poetic expression and can also be seen as a guidebook to follow your truth as you journey through life.

Dad's similarities to him show up in his own artistry; as a painter, drawer, photographer, singer and musician, he encouraged creativity of all forms and loved exploring history, nature, science, technology and diverse cultures around the world.

His values, morals, support of equality in all and commitment to the scales of justice, he was an outspoken hero in his own right.

As a loving and dedicated husband, father and grandfather and life of every family gathering; he had the courage to choose love, come to Canada, carve out his own noble and inspiring path and with his own iconic calligraphic penmanship; write his own story in life. His legacy lives on in his family today.

So proud of the essence of who they both were and what is yet to come as their stories will continue to be told.

Written by Umbereen Inayet (Great granddaughter) daughter of Mubaschir Inayet.

Award Winning Curator, Producer, Author and Cultural Strategist.

By Asad Abdullah

As a child, I have very fond memories of my grandfather - "aba-jaan" (Urdu for daddy dearest) as he was known to everyone in the family – from the many visits he made to our home in Karachi. Despite all the fame and wealth, I remember him to be a loving, simple man, invariably dressed in his signature white kurta and matching pajama's (straight pants) and grey Jinnah cap, sporting a contagious side smile, a style that was uniquely Hafeez Jalandhari.

My mother Shameem, was extremely proud of her father and loved him like no daughter had ever loved, till the time she passed away in December 2020. She would invariably pump up the television's volume whenever the national anthem was played, that showed her profound love and pride for her aba-jaan.

It was easily over 40 years ago that I recollect my mother asking my grandfather to write me a "shair" (a verse) for my keepsake. I remember moving at lightning speed to my room to grab a blue marker and some unlined paper, which I tore off a note book and dashed across to aba-jaan. Holding the marker between his index finger and clubbed thumb (which always fascinated me), a decent inch away from the tip, a style that was unique to him, I was in absolute awe to see him ink words before my eyes with fluidity and in a flash, there it was. My excitement was beyond words and why not. It's not every day that a young teenager gets lucky to not only have Hafeez Jalandhari as his grandfather but one who dedicates a shair – one that carried my name - exclusively to his grandson. Without doubt, I was the happiest and proudest kid.

As I grew, the reality slowly began to set-in that I was privileged to be the grandson of Hafeez Jalandhari. And you know what the best part is and one that I really enjoy, is to the see the expression on peoples faces change, when I tell them of my lineage. It's a real feel-good moment, one that undeniably leaves a lasting memory. Rest in eternal peace aba-jaan!

Asad Abdullah
Head Corporate Communications & CSR
Toyota, Pakistan

By Meeral Mughal

Tucked between the pages of Hafeez Jalandhari seminal epic poem Shahnama-e-Islam, I unexpectedly discovered a classic black and white photograph of my Nana. My mother must have slipped in that image of her beloved father decades ago. There was Abajaan, as he was reverently called, flashing a lopsided smile, resplendent in in his classic sherwani and Jinnah cap, leaning against the backdrop of my mom's lush garden in Karachi. That photo was most likely was taken on one of his many trips visiting his two daughters and extended family.

Those visits preceded regimental preparation and general humdrum under the watchful eye my mother Shameem, who I lovingly called "the Marshall law administrator". She had an uncanny way of anticipating her father's every need and went about delegating tasks to make his stay as comfortable as possible.

For an enormously famous man, my Nana was an unpretentious, down to earth personality. He had very specific every day needs and idiosyncrasies. He was not a big eater I remember, preferring daal and vegetables over red meat, and drinking tea especially brewed with Anise seeds, cardamon and a stick of cinnamon. The fragrance of which wafted through the house throughout his stay. His post dinner walks were a routine he seldom strayed from.

I do remember being quite shy and somewhat intimidated by his presence, so I mostly kept a low profile. Of course, like any curious kid I picked up on his daily habits. He spent most of the days reading and writing. I learnt from my mom that when he couldn't sleep which was often, he would scour through his already published literary work and rewrite some of the poems he felt could have been expressed with a bit more finesse. He would make those correction in the margins of those books. He never rested on his laurels but was always in the process of honing and evolving his artform.

We could occasionally hear him humming a tune under his breath, finding sudden inspiration in the world around him. His creative mind was never still or quiet. He was never idle. I once remember requesting a handwritten version of the Tarana,(the national anthem of Pakistan) he was happy to oblige. Regretfully I never followed through.

There is one other photograph I must mention; it's has made the several rounds over the social media, reaching me as messages from friends and acquaintances. Same lopsided smile, same Jinnah cap, in his signature kurta pajama, wearing worn shoes from all that walking he did, hitching a joyride on the back of the ubiquitous donkey cart.

Did I mention he was unpretentious. True poets, always are in search of human experiences which can be seen reflected in their poems. Poets are truth tellers and have strong, convictions and beliefs .They are revolutionaries.

How lucky are we to have been born into Hafeez Jalandhari's family. It is an honor and privilege to be associated with the author of the National Anthem of my beloved Pakistan; a nation he helped build with faith, honesty, integrity, and passion.

Meeral Mughal (Grand-daughter)

Hafeez Jalandhari enjoying a cart ride, Lahore

Hafeez Jalandhari Tomb, Lahore

XI

Hafeez Jalandhari photo gallery

11

A Journey Through Captured Moments

Each photo tells a story, a chapter in the epic saga of Poet Hafeez Jalandhari. As the pages turn, may these snapshots serve as windows into a life devoted to the pursuit of art, justice, and humanity.

As we leaf through the pages of Hafeez's life, each photograph holds a story, a memory frozen in time. The collection is part of Hafeez's personal collection; the poet documents the back of each photo with comments in Urdu, in his own handwriting. The collection of photos were handed down to the family with a profound wish that his journey be shared with the world. These images, like scattered pieces of a puzzle, form the tapestry of his existence – the journey of a poet, a patriot, and a humble servant of humanity.

In this dignified portrait, he stands tall, embodying the spirit of his beloved Pakistan. It symbolizes not just a man, but the aspirations of a nation striving for greatness.

More than mere snapshots, these portraits reflect the various facets of his identity as a poet and a citizen of Pakistan, each expression carrying a tale of its own.

Here, in the innocence of youth, he embarked on his poetic journey, reciting verses that would echo through the corridors of time. Brigadier Gulzar Ahmed's presence reminds him of the early support that fuelled his passion.

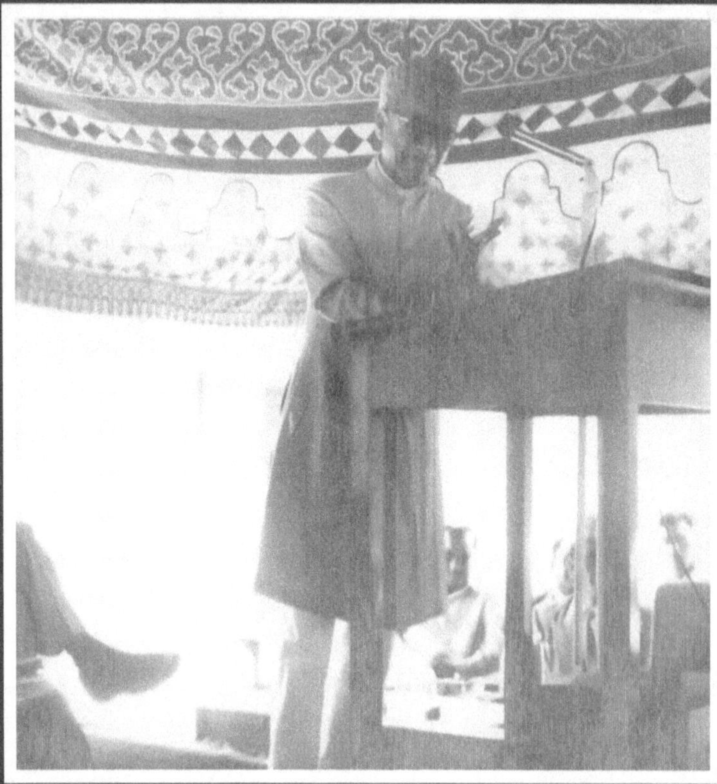

Amidst the gathering of fellow wordsmiths, he found solace and inspiration.
Here, in the company of Shamim Parneel and others, poetry transcends mere
words, forging bonds of camaraderie.

In the walled city of Lahore, he breathes life into the verses penned by his contemporaries, adding his voice to the chorus of literary giants who shaped the nation's cultural landscapes.

Education has always been close to Hafeez's heart. In this snapshot, he proudly stands alongside fellow advocates, united in a mission to empower the youth through knowledge.

As Director General of Village Aid, a philanthropy project, he embraced the noble cause of serving the underserved. At Layla Musa Center, they strived to uplift communities, embodying the principles of compassion and solidarity.

To be dubbed the "People's Poet" is a humbling honor. In 1964, he embraced this title with a sense of duty, recognizing the power of words to resonate with the masses.

Beyond borders, he ventured to Rangoon, where cultural exchange bridged divides. In 1957, he witnessed the universality of poetry, transcending linguistic and geographical barriers.

Surrounded by fellow luminaries, he shines amidst a constellation of talent. From Ustadi Azhar to Hafeez Ho Lia Uri, these poets and thinkers shaped the intellectual landscape of their era.

In the vibrant poetic events in Rangoon, he encountered kindred spirits like Hakeem Shahi and Sheikh Allah, whose friendship transcended borders, enriching his poetic journey.

Hospitality knows no bounds. In 1957, he welcomed an American filmmaker and his family into his home, fostering cross-cultural understanding amidst the backdrop of a philanthropy project-the Village Aid initiatives.

Education empowers minds and transforms societies. In 1962, he had the privilege of addressing the bright minds of Punjab University, igniting a passion for knowledge that would shape the future.

In the company of visionaries like Hakim Mohammed Saaed and Major General Fazal Muqeem Khan, he found himself humbled by their wisdom and inspired by their commitment to service.

United in their dedication to education, Dr. Masoud Al-Aqari, Hameed Ahmad Khan, and others join Hafeez in championing the cause of learning, knowing that knowledge is the key to progress.

Philanthropy knows no bounds. In this group photo, he stands shoulder to shoulder with fellow advocates, committed to making a difference in the lives of those less fortunate.

Diplomacy through dialogue. As he led a delegation to India, he sought to foster understanding and goodwill, believing in the power of dialogue to bridge divides and build bridges of friendship.

Amidst loved ones, Hafeez celebrates a milestone — the Golden Jubilee of a life dedicated to poetry, patriotism, and service. With daughters Fahmida and Shamim by his side, he reflects on a life well-lived, filled with moments of joy, sorrow, and everything in between.

Acknowledgements

I would like to express my heartfelt gratitude to those who played instrumental roles in the creation of this book.

Yvonne Christianson, for her invaluable guidance throughout the writing and editing process.

Marko Markovic, 5mediadesign, for his exceptional talent in book design and layout, which has brought the pages of this work to life with creativity and precision.

Yeon-Jeong Kim, for her meticulous oversight of the book's layout, ensuring its visual coherence and aesthetic appeal.

Ashraf Jalil Khan, for translations of Urdu documents and Haroon Rashid, for taking on any help needed for the project.

To family members, for contributing their thoughts and words to honor our beloved Abbajan.

In homage to our ancestors and dedication to a cherished grandchild:

Know deeply the sacred bond—
a timeless shield against the arrows of adversity
and a beacon of resilience
— Nanu

Ancestral Footsteps

Beneath the ancestral tree, where roots entwine,
Footsteps of ancestors in the sands of time.
Imprints in the earth, a path well-worn,
Guiding your journey, from dusk till dawn.

In the soft whispers of the rustling leaves,
Stories untold, a legacy that believes.
Follow the footsteps, as they gently sway,
Each print a tale, lighting your way.

Through the valleys of trials and heights so steep,
The echo of footsteps, a promise to keep.
In the tapestry of time, woven and spun,
Ancestors' footsteps, leading you as one.

Amidst life's labyrinth, where choices unfold,
The path of the past, a narrative told.
Follow the footprints, where love has trod,
A lineage of strength, connecting with God.

Through meadows of joy and storms that may sway,
The footsteps of ancestors pave your way.
Their love transcends, an eternal ray,
Guiding you through night into the day.

So, when the world seems harsh and skies turn grey,
Look to the ground where those footsteps lay.
In their silent wisdom, courage you find,
Ancestral footprints, in your heart entwined.

By Naveen Khan (Grand daughter)

9 781068 834813